To: Joe

D1617535

What People Are Saying:

I've been honored to know, serve along side, and walk through life with Jeremy Reynalds. And I can say unequivocally that two qualities characterize his life: One, Jeremy knows the depth of God's love for all people found in Christ; and, two, Jeremy knows that God's love in Christ compels him to serve others. It is this dual notion of salvation and service that has fueled his 30 years of ministry among the homeless of New Mexico—and through his writings—the homeless of the world.

God has used an English immigrant to help transform the landscape of an American city. Through the homeless shelter, Joy Junction, we here in Albuquerque, New Mexico are better because God commissioned—and continues to use—a man called for Christ.

So do yourself a favor: read Jeremy's newest book, *Two Hearts, One Vision*. And you never know, Christ may use you as a catalyst in our culture as He has Jeremy, engaging the world for eternity.

—Brian Nixon
Writer, Musician, and Minister

Jeremy Reynalds and those working at Joy Junction make the gospel visible by bringing a lifeline of hope to the homeless community. Joy Junction is both a sanctuary and a prayer in action and I have been moved to watch Jeremy over the years with this ministry that makes such a difference. Jeremy and his work at Joy Junction are a life changer.

—Canon Garth Hewitt
Singer/songwriter
Founder of social justice organization Amos Trust

In addition to his many responsibilities at Joy Junction, Jeremy Reynalds has been a senior correspondent for the ASSIST News Service (www. assistnews.net) for many years and is an excellent writer. While true, his life story reads like a novel, and makes for riveting reading. Once you have started it, you won't want to put it down. I am sure this is a book you will enjoy, for in it you will soon realize that Jeremy is making his life count for the Kingdom of God, and I pray that reading *Two Hearts, One Vision* will likewise inspire and encourage you to do the same.

—Dan Wooding
Author, broadcaster and journalist
Founder of the ASSIST News Service

Jeremy Reynalds is an iconociast who has combined a genuine passion for the hungry, homeless, abused, and addicted with a creative ministry model in New Mexico. His books give a face to what is often a faceless problem in today's society. This chronicle of his conversion, calling, and creation of an important agency of service—plus his guidelines for setting up a gospel rescue mission—is a valuable read for all who want to follow his lead and demonstrate their commitment to Jesus Christ in a practical manner.

—John Ashmen
President, Association of Gospel Rescue Missions

TWO HEARTS ONE VISION

HELPING THE HOMELESS TOGETHER

TWO HEARTS ONE VISION

HELPING THE HOMELESS TOGETHER

JEREMY REYNALDS Ph.D.

REDEMPTION
PRESS

© 2016 by Jeremy Reynalds. All rights reserved.

Published by Redemption Press, PO Box 427, Enumclaw, WA 98022 Toll Free (844) 2REDEEM (273-3336)

Redemption Press is honored to present this title in partnership with the author. The views expressed or implied in this work are those of the author. Redemption Press provides our imprint seal representing design excellence, creative content and high quality production.

All rights reserved. No part of this book may be used or reproduced by any means, graphic, electronic, or mechanical, including photocopying, recording, taping or by any information storage retrieval system without the written permission of the publisher except in the case of brief quotations embodied in critical articles and reviews.

Two Hearts, One Vision is a revised and expanded edition of *From Destitute to Ph.D.* © 2014, published by Redemption Press.

Because of the dynamic nature of the Internet, any web addresses or links contained in this book may have changed since publication and may no longer be valid. The views expressed in this work are solely those of the author and do not necessarily reflect the views of the publisher, and the publisher hereby disclaims any responsibility for them.

Although based on actual people and events, the specifics of some of the events and locations depicted in this book and the names of the characters involved have been changed to protect their identity and save them from any embarrassment.

All Scripture quotations, unless otherwise indicated, are taken from the Holy Bible, New International Version®, NIV®. Copyright ©1973, 1978, 1984, 2011 by Biblica, Inc.™ Used by permission of Zondervan. All rights reserved worldwide. www.zondervan.com

The "NIV" and "New International Version" are trademarks registered in the United States Patent and Trademark Office by Biblica, Inc.™ All rights reserved.

Scripture verses marked KJV are from the King James Version of the Bible.

Printed in the United States of America.

ISBN 13: 978-1-68314-063-4 (Print)
            978-1-68314-064-1 (ePub)
            978-1-68314-065-8 (Mobi)

Library of Congress Catalog Card Number: 2016945817

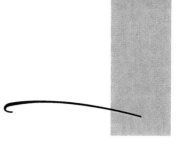

DEDICATION

Since *Two Hearts, One Vision* is the story of how the Lord worked in my life through taking me from a dark time to great joy that reawakened his original calling in my life, it is dedicated to him. Without the Lord, the ministry of Joy Junction would not have come into existence.

This book is dedicated to my amazing and beautiful wife, Elma, the "other" heart. She has shown me what it is to truly love and be loved.

This book is also dedicated to the many homeless men, women, and families who have met their Lord and Savior, Jesus Christ, and experienced his compassion while staying with us.

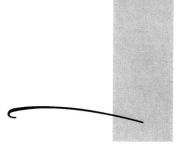

SPECIAL THANKS

Many thanks to the Joy Junction staff for carrying out the vision of homeless ministry on a daily basis.

My thanks also go to the late Bob Gassaway, formerly of the University of New Mexico, who has been a wonderful mentor and a good friend, and who gave me a lifelong appreciation of the importance of correct grammar.

FOREWORD

O nce in a while I come across a well written book that gets my attention.

I usually take my time to finish a book, but this time, I am surprised that I read a whole book in just two days. Yes, it's an easy reading, which is part the beauty of *Two Hearts, One Vision.*

It reminds me of those few adventure, love story books I read growing up. Jeremy's book gives us a wide variety of real stories of people finding hope in situations or circumstances that are seemingly hopeless. This book touched the core of my faith in God to fulfill His promises and I hope it does the same to you.

Two Hearts, One Vision is a story of love, adventure, courage and trust. It is a real account of lives touched by grace from struggles to victories. The book will change your perspective on homeless people and help you not to make quick judgments on people based on in their current situation, but rather be inspired to take steps to become part of their transformation. As a result, we will find ourselves changed for the better.

God's ability to engage and challenge each of us to participate is part of His desire for people to love, grow and appreciate the life He has entrusted to us. As I am inspired by this book, I hope you will be too.

Jeremy and his wife Elma are a match made in heaven. I've spent time with each of them, but hearing their separate stories is a great testament of God's sovereignty and how He worked and molded them for each other and for the ministry.

Two Hearts, One Vision shows a perfect second chance in love and purpose in life.

Jerome Bringas COO - The Edge Media Ministries
Davao, The Philippines

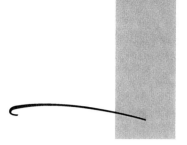

CONTENTS

Dedication vii

Special Thanks ix

Foreword xi

God's Unconventional Gift 1
    The Kiss of Hearts 3

A Reporter's Notebook 9

Homeless in America 15
    Growing Up in England 16
    The Gospel Hits Home 19
    Bible School 21
    America, Here I Come! 23
    A Different Side of the U.S. 27
    On the Road 29
    Food for Thought 31

Faltering First Steps 33
    A Learning Time 35

The "Almost Homeless" Former Shelter Operator 38

A New Home. 39

Crisis!. 40

Food for Thought. 43

The Promised Land **45**

Buying the Land. 46

More Land 50

Renovation. 52

Education for Excellence 54

The Tide of Time. 56

Struggling with Depression 58

Separation and Divorce 62

Food for Thought. 66

When Vision Becomes Reality **67**

Doing Everything at Once 69

The Homeless Speak **73**

A Common Scenario 73

A Family Shelter. 78

No Easy Fix, but Family's Commitment is Paying Off 79

Felicity. 82

Michael and Lucy 83

Charles and Nancy 83

Food for Thought. 84

Angels in Work Clothes: Meet Some of Our
Workers and Helpers **85**

From Addict to Chaplain 85

Macy and Gina, Formerly Homeless, Now Helpers 86

Harold, a New Life at Sixty-Nine. 88

Linus, Finding Meaning in Helping Others 92

Diana, Battling RA with a Brand New Attitude 96

Angels with Calculators: Free Tax Preparation from Phil's 97

An Angel Who Makes Residents Feel Safe:
Our Security Chief 100

Some People with Surprising Stories **103**
Mark 103
Beth, Billie, and Jenny 105
George 108
Fiona 109
Marsha 113
Raymond 115
Sheryl 117
Margie 120
Frank 122
Food for Thought. 124

To Worry or Not to Worry? That Is the Question **125**
Food for Thought. 127

When Poverty Knocks **129**
Food for Thought. 131

The Chicken, the Egg, and "Comorbidity" **133**
Knowing the Facts 136
Alcoholism and the Homeless: a Sin or a Disease? 138
Food for Thought. 140

Hunger Is Not Just Confined to One Cultural Group **141**
Food for Thought. 145

Not Your Typical Graduations **147**
Another Special CIPP Graduation 149
Food for Thought. 150

A Hand Up! **151**
Food for Thought. 153

Enduring a Walk of Shame **155**
Food for Thought. 157

Thanksgiving Memories **159**

Joy Junction's Thirtieth Thanksgiving 159

Thanksgiving: a Day of Both Sad and Happy Memories 161

Food for Thought. 164

Christmas at Joy Junction **165**

The Disappearing Diapers: A Higher Street
  Value Than Cocaine. 168

A Heartwarming Christmas Tale 169

Comments from Some Facebook Friends. 171

Food for Thought. 171

An Incredible Journey **173**

Day 1: The Journey Begins. 174

Day 2: The Incredible Journey Continues 177

Day 3: The Incredible Journey Concludes 178

Food for Thought. 179

Love and Help or Anger, Ridicule, and

Complaints: You Choose **181**

Actress from Down Under Thinks New Mexico Has a "Gummy"
  Problem 181

What Would You Do if This Was Your Last Day on Earth? . . 184

Albuquerque's Smelliest Problem 185

Food for Thought. 188

Who is Saying Bad Things about the Homeless? **189**

Mixing Religion with Delivery of Services 189

Johnny: "We Are Vapors" 191

Complaints About Crab Legs with Food Stamps? Hmmm . . . 194

Food Envy 196

Food for Thought. 197

Days and Nights on Albuquerque Streets **199**

Our Case Manager: A Day in the Life 201

Food for Thought. 204

Forty-Eight Hours at Joy Junction. **205**

Monday Afternoon. 205
Monday/Tuesday Graveyard Shift. 206
Tuesday 207
Tuesday/Wednesday Graveyard Shift 210
Wednesday. 211
Postscript 212
Food for Thought. 213

"Say My Name": The Homeless Are People, Not Statistics . . . 215
Vagrants Are People, Too 216
Joy Junction: Where Hope Outshines Fear. 219
Food for Thought. 221

"Those People Don't Want Help!" or Do They? 223
Food for Thought. 227

This is Our Life—Jeremy and Elma in Ministry 229

A Divine Appointment 233
Food for Thought. 234

You Can Never Get Taken Advantage of When You Give with the Right Attitude 235

Do Evangelicals Practice Compassion? 239
Bible Thumping the Homeless. 239
Building Relationships by Meeting Needs 241
Food for Thought. 243

Teachable Moments 245
Albuquerque Homeless Rate Drops—or Not? 245
So Who Are the Homeless in America? 248

What's Ahead for Joy Junction?. 251
Food for Thought. 253

About the Author. 255

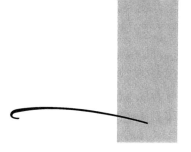

God's
Unconventional Gift
By Jeremy and Elma Reynalds

People "liking" Joy Junction on social media usually do so because they have a concern for the homeless and hungry and an appreciation for the help that community support allows us to give.

Each of our staff members at Joy Junction has a very personal story, and those stories greatly impact the work we do for the needy. As the founder and CEO of Joy Junction, I am no exception, and so I thought you may appreciate a peek behind the scenes at my life.

It's just over a year since I married Elma, the love of my life. She has quickly become an indispensable part of everything I do at Joy Junction, and we quickly realized that we are two hearts with one vision.

We're always together, where we're in the community daily, heightening awareness of the plight faced by the homeless and letting people know what they can do to make an impact on the issue by partnering with Joy Junction.

While I could never have kept going for so many years without your prayers and support, God also knew I needed a partner. As he told Elma shortly after we met, we could do more for him together than we could apart. We continue to see the truth of those words unfold daily.

In addition to our work for Joy Junction in the community, Elma and I usually finish our workdays off with a visit to the shelter. After all, that's ultimately the reason why we spend countless hours every day crisscrossing the streets of Albuquerque going from one meeting to another.

The time we spend at the shelter often includes some joking and light-hearted banter with the staff as well as interaction with our guests. As the months have gone by, they have come to increasingly love Elma. Who wouldn't? She's as lovely inside as she is out.

In addition, it's an absolute joy to spend many Saturday evenings sharing God's Word at Joy Junction with Elma concluding my message as she shares a five-to-ten-minute sermonette rounding out what I have been sharing. In addition, she occasionally blesses all of us with a song. She has a great voice. Of course, while our guests only get to hear her sing a song once, I am treated to her renditions many times as I hear her practicing.

The path to our getting married was not at all conventional. While beautifully covered by local media the day after we got married, some of you may not be aware of our journey.

So how did this whole adventure begin?

I first met Elma "virtually" on www.eHarmony.com in early 2013, and then in person in October 2013 during a quick trip to Israel. The following March I traveled to the Holy Land again as a reporter to cover the 2014 Christ at the Checkpoint Conference for the ASSIST News Service (ANS). Working with ANS and covering stories of this type is a natural extension of the ministry I feel God has given me to help bring light to the oppressed and marginalized.

The week at the conference was busy and eventful, as I'll relate in more detail in the next chapter. I interviewed several people with firsthand knowledge of the long history of the Israeli-Palestinian animosity, and I looked forward to the time I would spend with Elma in Tel Aviv. I could hardly wait to see her. We had talked daily on the phone, but we hadn't seen each other for several months.

Before leaving Bethlehem, however, there was one more "adventure" in store. I needed to get some money out of the ATM located in the hotel lobby. Two of the bills I got were 200 shekels each (almost $58). I did the transaction without a thought and put the bills in my wallet. A couple of days later while attempting to buy something in Tel Aviv with Elma, a clerk looked at the bills and told me they were fake. The paper was much glossier and of a lower grade than the genuine article. I would have never thought I could get fake money from an ATM! I should have known better.

Elma and I had a wonderful time of reconnecting from Friday afternoon through Monday evening. The highlight was an engagement dinner for us on Sunday night at The Old Man and the Sea restaurant in Jaffa Port with a number of friends from Elma's church family, including her pastors. They went out of their way to embrace me and make me feel welcomed and loved, which I most definitely did. What a delight it was to experience God's plan and redemption unfold for me in my personal life!

The Kiss of Hearts

A year back before Elma and I met on eHarmony, we each had been praying that God would bring the right person into our lives—not only as husband or wife, but also as a ministry partner. We had both learned (after many years) to give God the full authority over our lives in finding that person. Doing so always works out best in the end, and Elma and I are ongoing testimonies of that fact.

We are both Christians and love to help the poor, hungry, marginalized, and disenfranchised. What better choice for a life partner than that? We got engaged in Bethlehem and returned to Tel Aviv a few days later.

When it was time to leave Israel the following week, tears flowed. I realized I was truly in love and had met the woman with whom I wanted to spend the rest of my life. During the ensuing months we continued to talk daily, usually for between ninety minutes to two hours at a time. I spent more time with Elma on the phone than I had with anyone else in my life.

Of course, that was all we *could* do. We couldn't go out to see a movie or take a walk on the beach. However, that time we spent talking laid a great foundation for a strong relationship. Most married couples don't spend that amount of time communicating. When I would sometimes tell friends how long we talked on the phone, they would look at me in amazement. We talked about every subject conceivable, including sharing what we imagined our lives together would be like in the years ahead. There was no made-for-TV drama in our deepening relationship. Instead, there was an increase in the love and commitment we felt for each other.

In January 2014, I had already submitted a packet of information to the U.S. government to start the ball rolling for the K-1 visa—also referred to as the "90-day fiancé visa"—upon which the TLC reality show of the same name is based. There are differences between our experience and the experiences of the show's participants, though: *90 Day Fiancé* focuses outward on the drama that occurs after the foreign fiancé arrives in the United States. In our case, however, the drama was more internal as we worked our way through the visa process and exposed much of our lives to the probing eyes of the U.S. government. In addition to tax returns, fingerprints, an FBI background check, and proof of income, Elma and I also had to include, as part of our application package, a number of the e-mails we had exchanged with each other.

While, technically, the requirement for a K-1 visa is that you only have to meet once in person preceding the interview at the embassy, obviously more meetings are conducive to a healthy relationship. They're also useful to help prove the relationship is genuine to routinely suspicious consular officials.

In July 2014, Elma returned to the Philippines to spend some time with her daughter. I joined her a few weeks later, and we started gathering additional documents still needed for the all-important interview at the embassy, for which we still didn't have a date.

As we waited and waited, we both felt frustrated and powerless. We couldn't do anything other than let the wheels of the bureaucratic process run their course. And for me, typically a type-A personality, it was perhaps worse than for someone with a more low-key, relaxed personality. I would wake up day after day hoping there would be some communication indicating progress. Elma encouraged me to be patient. I wasn't.

Finally, we found out that the U.S. Embassy in Manila was ready for us to schedule our appointment. We went online and saw that January 29, 2015 was available. After that, I recall, there was nothing open for at least a couple of months. We quickly locked in the date.

The day loomed large in our minds. As it drew closer, neither Elma nor I thought about much else. We were prayerfully prepared, but it was still a tense time.

Finally the day arrived. Elma went by herself to the interview, as we didn't think I was allowed to be there with her. (Later on, I found that I could have accompanied her.)

The morning hours of January 29 passed slowly for me, as I prayed and waited for Elma to come back and tell me how things had gone. Finally she arrived and said that things had gone well, but we still needed three more documents. Two of those we obtained the same day and sent to the embassy; another one took a little longer. About a couple of weeks later we heard from the embassy that they had everything the staff needed and would notify us of their decision.

We were back to the waiting game again, and there was nothing else for us to do other than wait. During those weeks I appreciated our good friends in Davao who encouraged us during this time, as they had for many months prior. The Edge radio station manager Jay Bringas, Pastor Michael Thompson, and Jeremiah Gubat, you will always have a special place in our hearts.

That long anticipated e-mail arrived from the embassy a couple of weeks or so after. Elma had been granted the K-1 visa. I started crying—tears of happiness. Our long wait was over.

As I reflect on the last three years, I realize they have been the most exciting time in my life. God used the eHarmony computers to introduce us to each other, and that resulted in me getting to know the woman who would become the love of my life and very soon my wife.

Thanks to God's provision and the Holy Spirit's unifying gift, we are now two hearts with one vision for the homeless, poor and hungry.

"True Love Starts with the Kiss of Hearts," says the song of that name by Christian musicians Steve and Annie Chapman. It goes on to say, "Though a kiss may be the end result, it should never be the reason."

That's the way it happened for my wife Elma and me. We've now been married just over a year and are savoring every minute. It all started with the "kiss of hearts."

Remembering how our relationship grew, I recall how we talked about every subject conceivable, including sharing what we imagined our lives together would be like in the years ahead. We also shared past experiences in our lives that had led us to where we are today—together in love and ministry.

Knowing and loving Elma has caused me to marvel as I have asked myself what makes the "other heart" of Joy Junction beat with such a resounding passion for the needy? In addition to being an obvious spiritual gift, from where did Elma's compassion come in a human sense? I had never met anyone in my life as Elma who is as moved by and interested in bettering the plight of the needy, hungry, and disenfranchised.

I knew her life growing up in the Philippines was far from easy. Her parents, while both hardworking farmers, often struggled to make ends meet. Elma said they had three meals a day "most of the time," but when her parents got sick, finding the necessary funds to go to the doctor was a challenge.

Those hardships helped instill in Elma an ongoing desire to work hard to help ensure she had a better life, as well as to help her family and other people in need who she encountered.

Elma's parents always reminded her to be kind and compassionate to the less fortunate. She says, "Both of them had a big heart. They always helped others, even when we only had enough for us."

Fast forward to Elma becoming a caregiver in Israel for nearly twenty years. Due to the wages available in the Philippines (a typical wage may be a dollar an hour or a little more), it's a common practice for many Filipinos to spend a lot of their working life outside the country and to send much of their income back home to support family. Elma says the almost two decades she spent in Israel helped mold her further into the person she is today.

She was able to meet some needs. Over a decade ago, her sister who is a pastor of a church in a rural area of the Philippines, told her about a woman who was in immediate need of an operation in her right eye or she would probably end up going blind in both. Despite the offer of a free operation, additional funds were needed to make the procedure a reality.

Thinking about the need, Elma was unable to sleep until she gave what she had saved to allow the operation to happen. Three years later while visiting the Philippines, Elma met the woman, who thanked her for the generosity that allowed her to live a normal life.

"Her story opened my eyes by being sensitive to other people needs," Elma explains. "It was so scary for me to think if I didn't pay attention when the Lord was leading me to help that woman, she would have been blind by the time I met her in person."

Elma continues, "Though I learned to love my job and was contented with my life, I knew there was something more out there God had in store for me, but I had no clue what it was."

In late 2012, Elma felt she wanted to be in a ministry that fed the hungry with three meals a day, helped the poor and homeless, and ensured that youngsters could go to school with the school supplies they needed.

She knew this was a very ambitious goal, but she was also aware that nothing was impossible with God. "All I could do was pray and ask God to lead me to the direction where He wanted me to go. The best thing that happens when you just continue to delight yourself in the Lord, is that he will give you the desire of your heart."

On March 27, 2015, following an amazing adventure and a number of challenges, we became husband and wife. I have shared a shortened version of my article, "Two Hearts, One Vision," which appears earlier in this chapter (www.joyjunction.org/two-hearts-one-vision/).

Having a shared vision has been both challenging and rewarding. "We both wake up thinking about Joy Junction, spend the whole day working for JJ, and the last thing in our mind before going to bed is still JJ," Elma says, echoing my own thoughts. She adds, "We're dealing with different kinds of people at JJ, but at the same time, I never have trouble in understanding the needs of the people we serve. I understand exactly what our guests are dealing with. Many of them are not hesitant to come and talk to me and are so grateful that I am willing to listen and encourage them."

Looking back, Elma says she is amazed at what God has done—and keeps doing—as am I. I am humbled and honored to be one of two hearts with the same vision. Elma now understands why she's always had a heart for the needy. "Everything I have experienced in my life prepared me for the ministry where God has put me. Now I feel whole and complete in my life."

Meeting Jesus in 1976 changed my life forever. Now forty years later, my journey with the most amazing woman I have ever met in my life is everything I ever thought it could be and more. I wake up each morning thankful for the blessings God has given me. I look forward to what lies ahead as I go about the day's activities with Elma at my side.

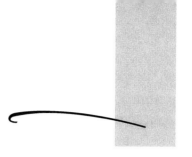

A REPORTER'S NOTEBOOK

As a reporter, I keep notes about the backstories related to the ones I submit. Following is my reporter's notebook of the trip that cemented Elma's and my future:

I left Albuquerque for Washington's Dulles Airport, from which my journey began with an uneventful flight to Munich. I arrived at Ben Gurion Airport just after 2:00 p.m., which would have been 6:00 a.m. Albuquerque time.

After navigating through Israeli immigration, I went to the airport entrance where I found a cab I had booked in advance. We started out for the beautiful hotel facility where the conference was to be held. I checked into my room and took a few moments to breathe.

After cleaning up, I followed directions through the cavernous hotel to find out where dinner was being served. At my best I am directionally challenged, and that's in places I know. This hotel posed a special challenge. But once I got my footing and found where I was supposed to be heading, I met some delightful United Methodists from Oklahoma who were there for the conference.

By dinner's end, I was exhausted and the pillow was calling my name. I got up late the next morning, had some Turkish coffee (my favorite), and did some pre-conference interviews with attendees willing to talk to me.

At lunch, someone tapped me on the shoulder. It was a pleasure to run into Isam Ghattas, director of Manara Ministries in Amman, Jordan. I met Isam some years before while in Jordan for ANS. We caught up a bit, and I also enjoyed meeting his wife. They are an amazing couple. Among other things, Manara helps refugees who have flooded into Jordan from neighboring countries.

A while later, the Christ at the Checkpoint Conference opened with a word of greeting from Rev. Munir Kakish, president of the Evangelical Council in Palestine. He said, "As a religious group, we are unable to practice our civil rights . . . Our council prays for peace and justice to rule our land." Then World Evangelical Alliance CEO, Rev. Dr. Geoff Tunnicliffe, also greeted delegates. He began by requesting official recognition of his group's member churches from the Palestinian Authority, adding, "I will bring the same message to Israel later this week." Tunnicliffe concluded by saying, "My hope and prayer is that as evangelicals, we can be on the leading edge of peace, so that in coming years there may be a new bridge of peace."

After the opening session concluded, I went outside the hotel where the evening traffic was quite brisk. There was nothing visible occurring out of the ordinary. The traffic flowed, and people walked in and out of local stores buying necessities. It occurred to me this scene could have been played out almost anywhere in the world.

Just a few hundred yards from the hotel, however, was a quiet reminder of what the conference was all about. A sign read, "Warning. This is illegally occupied land. State of Palestine." Never forget, this is an area in the Holy Land where ongoing tension bubbles just beneath the surface—and sometimes spills right over. Thus the reality of the tense Middle East situation was brought right home for me and other conference delegates.

When the morning session concluded, a conference organizer told those interested in eating lunch at the nearby Bethlehem Bible College (organizers of the conference) they needed to take a back door from the hotel, as there was an "incident" occurring outside in the front. Undeterred, I ran out to see what was going on. Bethlehem's main street was full of choking tear gas and rubber bullets as the Israeli army faced off against stone-throwing Palestinian youth.

An observer told me about one hundred young people were involved, upset about what they believed was the killing of at least two Palestinians by the Israeli army (IDF) in the few days prior to the conference. The reason for the killing was disputed— depending on which narrative you listen to—that of the Israelis or the Palestinians.

One side of the story, represented by a *Times of Israel* article, said, according to a *Ma'an News* report, driver Fidaa Muhye Addin Majadlah was killed and passenger Ibrahim Adnan Shukri was seriously injured after their car went off the road and flipped over. The other side of the story was that the Israeli Defense Forces (IDF) had shot the men.

The *Times* said while a Palestinian security source had initially told the news service AFP that IDF forces had fired on the vehicle, the news agency retracted the story after Palestinians notified them that "their information on army gunfire was incorrect."

The young people involved in the demonstration outside the hotel were also reportedly upset about the killing of a judge by the IDF at the Allenby Crossing. While a preliminary IDF investigation said that an IDF soldier fired his weapon because he felt his life was in danger, Palestinians weren't buying it.

According to a story by Gili Cohen and Jack Khoury for *Haaretz*, the Jordanian government sent a sharply worded statement to Israel following the killing of the judge. The border terminal is operated jointly by Israel, Jordan, and the Palestinian Authority. It is the main border crossing for Palestinians from the West Bank traveling to neighboring Jordan and beyond and a crossing point for goods between Israel, the West Bank, and Jordan.

Officials in Jordan told *Haaretz* the government is under pressure to conduct an in-depth investigation, and that the issue would be discussed in parliament.

Though hotel security ushered us back in (or tried to), I stayed outside the hotel as close as I could to everything going on. I appreciated their concern for our safety, but I felt compelled to observe the melee firsthand. The tear gas was thick, and I really didn't want to inhale its obnoxious fumes, yet I needed to find out what it felt like. Just a few short whiffs were enough as the gas made its way to the back of my throat, stung my eyes, and gave me a gigantic headache. An ambulance made its way down the street past the hotel. I heard a Palestinian youngster had inhaled too much of the tear gas and needed medical treatment.

Regardless of your political viewpoint on who is "right" and who is "wrong," can you imagine living like this? I was told that similar situations are a pretty regular occurrence in Bethlehem.

More conference sessions came and went, and there were a multitude of viewpoints presented. One influential college president did not seem be a good judge of his audience when he told everyone he felt safer since the wall, or checkpoint, was built. A torrent of disagreement rippled through the audience when he said that.

On the afternoon of the third day of the conference, I visited a longtime friend in Bethlehem, Joseph Canavati, owner of the Alexander Hotel, where I had stayed in previous years. Joseph has always been so gracious to me. He set me up with a couple of interviews last year that included a visit to one of Bethlehem's hugely overpopulated refugee camps, Camp Aida.

It was so good to reconnect again and enjoy Turkish coffee with Joseph, his wife Ivonne, and their son Joey. Since I brought only three shirts on the trip with me, I asked Ivonne if she had any idea where I could get some shirts, thinking she would direct me to a local store. But she was kind enough to give me some, which lessened my predicament and ensured I wouldn't be a smelly distraction to those around me!

The next day at the conference brought a message from Pastor Bob Roberts who energized delegates right from his opening words. Later, he was gracious enough to give me a one-on-one interview. Roberts is the founder and senior pastor of Northwood Church near Dallas, Texas. He covered a number of issues in his conference presentation, including the fact that he loves both his Jewish friends and his Palestinian friends. When he asked conference delegates how many of them love Israel and pray for the peace of Jerusalem, there was loud applause. Roberts also spoke about eschatology (events associated with the end times). He apologized to Palestinians on this topic, saying his heart breaks for their suffering.

"Pray for the peace of Jerusalem," Psalm 122:6 instructs. We can each do that, no matter what our political or religious persuasions are.

And we can pray for each other. Elma and I appreciate your prayers and support as we continue together with the work that God has for us. I'll shortly elaborate on that work, or rather, "calling," but first, let me relate how God taught me what being homeless is like—by allowing me to experience it for myself.

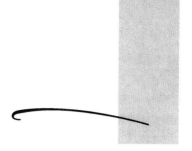

HOMELESS IN AMERICA

I was not on a mission for God. I was just a broke young Englishman stranded in the American Southwest. I had made it to the New Mexico-Texas border but ended up standing in the blazing sun for hours. Cars sped by, but none stopped. As the hours passed, I was getting more and more tired, so I left the highway and walked to a store. I wearily looked through a telephone directory and called the first church I could find. I then asked the man who answered the phone if he could help me find shelter. The man told me I was welcome to sleep on the church floor, but I would have to walk there—a distance of about five miles. Needless to say, walking that far on an unknown Texas highway was more than my body or spirit could endure. I thanked him and dejectedly hung up.

Walking back, I saw a restaurant that was about to close for the night. It didn't matter, because I had no money for food. I saw behind the restaurant there was a storage shed filled with odds and ends, and I looked for something to sleep on. The only thing that looked suitable was a piece of fiberglass, and that was my bed for the night.

I woke up early the next day and headed down the highway again. Soon, a trucker stopped and gave me a ride to Phoenix. By this time, I was starving. Without me asking, the kind trucker shared his sandwiches with me. Looking back all these years later, I see the Lord's hand in my life. Back then I was just another homeless person on the road. Today I am founder and CEO of Joy Junction, New Mexico's largest emergency homeless shelter. The transformation came through God's grace in my life.

Growing Up in England

My heart pounded as I lay in bed and listened to the muffled, angry voices coming from the living room. My mother and father were arguing again. About what I did not know. I just knew they were fighting, something they did almost every night. I was eleven, and I hated listening to my parents' fights. I knew my mother was unhappy living with my wheelchair-bound father, diagnosed several years earlier with multiple sclerosis. On a number of occasions, she acidly told me if my dad had not been sick, she would have left him. At other times, Mom informed me I should be grateful she stuck around to take care of my older brother and me. Lots of parents would not have done that, she said. My mother only married my father because he told her he would apply for a commissioned officer's position in Britain's Royal Air Force. He failed to do so, and now, because of his disability, there was no chance of that. She felt cheated and angry.

As sharp tones filtered through the muffled voices, I focused on the one bright spot on the horizon: I would be leaving for boarding school in a few weeks. Initially, I looked forward to this as an escape, but later it became my own private hell.

At boarding school in Bournemouth, only about an hour's bus ride from my home on England's south coast, I was the routine victim of schoolboy pranks, such as having my bed short-sheeted. Days were filled with dread, as I worried about being laughed at for my stammering when asked to give an impromptu answer. If that wasn't enough, there was also the necessity of faking a sickness to escape the perils of hockey games, rugby football, cricket, or cross-country running—all nightmares for my un-athletic body and so much fun for others to laugh at. I didn't seem to fit in anywhere, so I retreated into a world of books where no one demanded anything from me. This traumatic time was perhaps the beginning of my shutting down emotionally. The pain of being continually taunted by a multitude of pampered and merciless British kids was too much for me to bear.

Ironically, my escape on many weekends was to go back to the home from which I had tried to escape. Perhaps I concluded the tension at home was somewhat bearable compared to the abject misery I endured at school.

Admittedly, there were a few fun times at school. One early morning, all the kids in my dorm awoke at about two o'clock, buzzing with excitement. The chapel was on fire. Since a destroyed chapel meant no church services in the morning, and maybe for a long time, the kids were elated. Those chapel services were extremely boring for me—just something else in my life to be endured rather than enjoyed. The fire and the circumstances surrounding it were the talk of the campus, and did we love what we found out!

The word was the school chaplain had gone for an evening of entertainment in a nearby town. Returning to school (where he lived) in the early hours of the morning, he found the chapel on fire. This hip spiritual adviser had not gone to town dressed in robe and cassock, however. He dressed in full sixties regalia, including a Beatles-style wig and high-heeled boots. Naturally, we all thought this was hilarious. No one talked about anything else for days.

I scarcely remember anything about most of my classes and my teachers. There was one very memorable class I attended, however, even though I hated it. It was math class, and my teacher, a born-again Christian, is someone I have never forgotten. The last few math lessons of each semester were different. For a treat at the end of each term, this teacher asked if we would like him to read to us. Naturally we agreed, even though we thought his choice of books could have been improved (but then, anything beat math!). His readings of choice were evangelical Christian books, usually dramatic life stories about a hero of the Christian faith who had done exciting things for the Lord. While I did not at that time know the author of the Good Book, the stories were very gripping and easily held my attention.

I took it on myself to argue with this teacher about whether Christianity was relevant to culture. I was then a vegetarian, and I had read books saying Jesus didn't eat meat, either. I used those books as weapons to argue with him, and I twisted Scripture in any way I could to persuade him.

Instead of falling for my arguments, this godly man responded that the important thing was not what Jesus ate but what he had done for me on the cross. I let my long-suffering instructor know Christianity was a crutch for old women and the intellectually feeble. How difficult it must have been for this man to deal with my obstinacy! Still, those powerful, end-of-term stories remained with me, as did my memories of this faithful, patient teacher.

I wanted to study sociology, a subject not offered at my boarding school, so I finished the last couple of years of my education living at home again. I still did not fit in. I attended a different school, with different people, but I encountered the same misery. I was desperately lonely and felt like an outsider again. I threw myself into my studies, and soon I adopted all the latest sociological buzzwords and phrases into my vocabulary. One such phrase was Karl Marx's well-known saying, "Religion is the opiate of the people."

I remember scoffing at various religious posters I saw plastered around town. I proudly declared, "I am not a Christian. I am an agnostic. You can't tell if there is a God." My mother was bitterly angry about this, but I reasoned that if the Bible was not true (and I had already made up my mind that it was not), then Christianity was false, since the Bible is its foundation.

Desperate for friends, I eagerly welcomed attention of any type. One day I was sitting in the student lounge when an attractive young woman came up to me and started talking. Her name was Jenny Griffith. There was a hook to the conversation, however. Jenny was a Christian and she invited me to church. I did not relish the prospect, but I definitely liked the idea of seeing more of Jenny, so I went. Was I in for a shock! This was not like anything I had imagined, for my idea of church was based on very formal, proper, incense-burning Anglican parishes. This church was not like that at all. It was very small, and it had no organ. There were seats instead of pews. The congregation sang lively, upbeat songs and sounded as if they actually enjoyed being there. Everyone was very friendly. Surprisingly, I liked it. This was definitely unlike any other type of church or religious organization I had ever encountered.

I continued returning to this small, friendly, and informal little church—although not for the right reasons. I was hoping there might be the possibility of a relationship springing up between Jenny and me. The Lord, meanwhile, had other more significant things in mind, beginning with my salvation!

The Gospel Hits Home

Following one Sunday night service, the pastor of the little church approached me and asked if I wanted to do anything "about it." I asked him what "it" was, and he again responded by asking if I wanted to do anything "about it." I told him I was not interested in "it," and that, for the moment, was the end of the conversation. It was not until later that I learned Pastor Phillip Powell was really asking me if I wanted to commit my life to Jesus Christ. He did not want to be overly pushy and force the situation, hence the mystery about "it." He felt if he came on too strong it might cause me to run out the door and never come back.

As the weeks went on, I continued attending church, and I even started listening to contemporary Christian music at home. I was also developing an interest in what the pastor was saying. It seemed the

Lord's hook had caught another fish, and it was time to reel it in. While initially attending church to spend more time with Jenny rather than to learn about Jesus, as I heard the Word preached and taught, it now began to take effect.

One day I purchased a copy of *Good News for Modern Man*, a modern translation of the Bible. For the first time, I read Scripture with an open mind. Instead of considering myself to be so intellectually superior that the Bible had nothing to teach me, I read it with a sincere interest in knowing what it said about who God is. I picked up that book and said, "God, if you're real, please speak to me in a way I can understand."

At that point, I can honestly say I had a genuine, supernatural experience. The letters on the Bible page in front of me appeared to be about six feet tall. From that point on, I read Scripture with a different set of eyes: the eyes of understanding that God gave me. And I knew what I read was true. I asked God to intervene in my life in a way I could grasp, and he honored my request.

He will do the same for anyone who asks him. The Word of God says, "If from there you seek the LORD your God, you will find him if you look for him with all your heart and with all your soul" (Deut. 4:29). That happened to me over thirty years ago, and it was a supernatural experience, a one-of-a-kind encounter where God met me where I was at that time in my life. Although I have had other supernatural experiences, nothing quite like that one has occurred since. That was the coup de grâce. My relationship with the Lord has deepened over the years, and he has communicated with me in many different ways—but nothing quite so dramatically as that time.

Despite that extraordinary incident, I was still not on board with trusting Jesus as my Savior. I had not completely surrendered my life to his control, but the Lord was supernaturally preparing my heart to do so. I did not even know how to "get saved." A week later, however, I was reading a book by an Anglican clergyman named David Watson. He made a very simple, yet profoundly compelling statement to the effect that if you have never asked Jesus Christ to be your Lord and Savior, you are not a Christian, and you will be eternally lost.

My newfound understanding of the truth of the Bible swept away any reasons to hesitate. At that moment, I bowed my head and asked Jesus Christ to be the Lord of my life. There were no flashing lights and no further supernatural experiences, only a quiet act of obedience to God's Word. At that point, the future direction of my life became clearer. I was a Christian, and God was beginning an exciting work in me, preparing me for something I could hardly imagine.

Becoming a Christian brought with it certain profound changes in my personality and behavior. My mother began noticing those transformations in me and became rather worried about my sudden religious "fanaticism." She was not overly concerned about the changes she saw at first, because she thought it was just another phase I was going through and that I would get over it. But as my faith solidified and began increasing rather than dissipating, she became very concerned indeed. She even went so far as to make an appointment for me with a local Anglican parish priest. He asked me if I really thought anyone who did not receive Jesus Christ as his Lord and Savior would go to hell. Assuring him I most definitely believed just that, he terminated the interview, shaking his head in absolute disbelief. He thought there was no hope for me, but I had an eternal hope by the name of Jesus.

Bible School

I felt the need to receive some Bible college instruction, so I spent the 1976–1977 academic year at a Bible college in South Wales. It was a good experience for the most part, like being in a spiritual hothouse. After finishing that year, I returned home to Bournemouth where the burning question became what I planned to do with my life. As I prayed, I began to feel God might be calling me to full-time ministry. That was a challenge for me then. The church in England where I met Christ did not give young people the opportunity to make their own decisions about obeying God's calling in their lives. In other words, you were not encouraged to decide individually to obey God. Instead, someone who had more spiritual authority had to decide for you. Still, I followed the call as I heard it by applying to a couple of universities as well as to London Bible College.

I was accepted at LBC, but shortly thereafter, I sensed a call from God to go to the United States. I applied to Southeastern College in Lakeland, Florida, and was initially accepted. That was only the beginning. There were still lots of other issues to be worked out, such as how I planned to pay for everything. While England was very generous in student financial aid, that generosity only extended to those attending British colleges and universities. The British government was not willing to finance a student going to school in the United States. This meant I was at a standstill: unemployed with an acceptance to an American college valid only if I could come up with the funds to get there and subsequently support myself.

Meanwhile, things were a little rocky at church youth group meetings, where I soon became the object of humor—especially when there were guest speakers. When other young people introduced themselves to guests and said what they did for a living, they would laughingly say about me, "Oh, that's Jeremy Reynalds, and he's going to America!" The months dragged on, and I was not any closer to getting over the pond. Had I missed God's calling in my life? Should I abandon the entire plan?

I was on the verge of giving up my idea to emigrate to the United States when, a few weeks later, something very interesting happened. I had been corresponding with a minister who had previously spent some time in the United States, and he invited me to meet him. Consequently, a few weeks later, I took the train from Bournemouth to London, a journey of about one hundred miles, to meet with this individual. I told him all my woes, hoping he might offer me some money. He did not. Instead, he told me, "Jeremy, you say God has called you to America. But right now you have a lot of time on your hands. I wish I had the amount of time you do. Go home and make up your mind that you are going. If you say God has told you, then act on it." This man's sound advice caused a change in my thinking. God used his words to speak deeply to my heart, and I knew from then on that I would be crossing the pond to America.

America, Here I Come!

Three days after meeting with the minister in London, a lady asked me how my plans to go to the United States were going. She did not profess any relationship with Christ, but I knew her through some friends. After I told her I was going no matter what, she gave me two hundred dollars for the airfare. Ten days later I was offered a place to stay in Orlando, Florida, by an English pastor and his wife who opened their home to me without even knowing who I was.

I was on the plane two weeks after this. Even though I was actually flying across the Atlantic, it was still hard for me to believe what I had dreamed of, hoped for, and prayed about for so long was becoming a reality. What was in store?

I might not have been so keen to go had I known. In time, what awaited me was poverty, homelessness, almost losing my ministry, and an eventual divorce. All that and more came later, but one thing I learned right off the bat was it was time for me to grow up. I was on my own now. For the previous twenty years, I had lived a relatively pampered life with a guaranteed roof over my head and three meals a day. Whether I worked really made no difference. Now things had changed, and it was just the Lord and me. I knew I would have to take care of myself.

Just before I left for the States, my mother said I was making my bed and would have to lie in it, meaning I would face all the consequences of choosing to leave England. She made it quite clear there would be no help from her at all. She had done enough, and now, she said, I was denigrating all her assistance by going to the Colonies (as she dubbed the United States) on a "wild-goose chase." And it was all because of that "fanatical religion."

She did have some reason for the way she felt. My mother had taken wonderful care of my older brother, Tony, and me. We both benefited from her tutelage and strong English private school educations. Mom felt she had prepared us properly, and I admit I was less than gracious and wise in my comments to her since my conversion.

For example, one morning we were in a heated argument. I told this good, upright, caring Englishwoman she was both a heathen and a sinner! Now, from a scriptural point of view, this was perhaps true. But saying so, and saying so in the way I did, was unkind and unwise. To my mother, a sinner was someone like a prostitute, and a heathen was a half-naked person running around a jungle. To put the matter delicately, my newfound Christian zeal needed some refining!

Thankfully, God worked in me to develop the wisdom and compassion I lacked. I can look back now and see some of the experiences ahead of me were the Lord's way of preparing me for my work of ministering to the poor and needy. How wonderful God is to weave into our lives the very circumstances he will use to enable us to serve him.

I arrived at Miami International Airport clutching my one-way ticket to America carrying my last fifty dollars in my pocket. At that time in 1978, an Air Florida ticket from Miami to Orlando only cost twenty dollars. Haven't times changed! I was in the United States with thirty dollars in my pocket, and this represented all my worldly wealth.

I disembarked from the plane and made my way to immigration. There were numerous booths from which I could choose, so I prayed and made my selection. I knew I needed to trust God in this and all things, although I did not always do so—to my detriment.

The official at the booth asked me what I planned to do while I was in the United States and how long I wanted to stay. When I told him I wanted to preach the gospel, he looked a little concerned and asked, "Oh, are you going to make a living at that? There are people who make a lot of money doing that." I don't know if he was being cynical or serious.

Years later I realized how the Lord had gone before me during that experience when I learned what the official should have asked me. He should have asked me if I had a return air ticket to England. If I could not produce one, he should have inquired if I had enough money to purchase one. That would have been protocol. Fortunately for me, he did not ask those things. It seems the Lord was serious about taking a middle-class English boy with absolutely no personal experience of being poor, hungry, and homeless and sending him to the United States to help care for America's needy.

Finally, I arrived at the pastor's house in Orlando. A lady answered the door, introduced herself as Julie, and said her husband would be back shortly. She gave me tea (naturally, she was English). When her husband, Phil, arrived, they questioned me closely about my plans and then said something that chilled me. It impacted me so greatly I still remember it as clearly today as the day it was spoken.

Phil said, "Our faith has gotten us here, and if you want to get anywhere, it's going to have to be your faith that does it. You're not going to sponge off us, okay?"

With a mouth that went instantly dry, I gulped a quick response, assuring the couple I would not sponge off them. What else was I going to say? Yet I was now in a foreign country, staying with strangers, and U.S. immigration law prevented me from working while holding a visitor's visa. I had nothing. I was very much like the homeless people I would be helping some years down the road: totally dependent on others for my most basic needs.

Phil and Julie's reception and attitude was not quite what I had expected, and I was caught up short. All sorts of things flooded through my mind during the next few minutes. Maybe I could go back to England without losing too much face and reapply to London Bible College. Maybe . . . maybe . . . maybe. I was still trying to determine just exactly what I had really gotten myself into when the couple said they were really tired and showed me my room. I went to bed.

I lay in bed for a long time that night, thinking and wondering.

It was obvious this couple was not going to give me a free ride just because I said God had called me to America. If God really had called me, they wanted to see some proof.

The next day I could see more trouble brewing on the horizon when, in an expanded version of what they had already told me, they said, "You say God has called you to America. Well, he has called us as well. You are in our house, which is a tangible example of God providing for us. It has a pool and orange trees, and we have plenty of food in our pantry. If God has called you, he will provide for you as well."

I was getting more fearful by the minute. It is one thing to tell your peers in England God has called you to another country. It sounds sort of grand, even if they do not believe you. But, all the while I was telling them, I was still being provided for by my parents. Now, God would have to be my provider. If he did not, starvation or deportation was imminent, and those things were all I could think of.

A couple of days passed before I made my first visit to an American church. While I did not know it, sitting in that service was my future wife. But that was not the thing I remember about the service—in fact, I don't even remember seeing her at the time. Neither was the sermon or the church building the thing I remembered from that first service. As odd as it may seem, it was learning the church had a secretary. This was my first real sense that I was being exposed to the American church culture, and it was a shock. All the evangelical churches I had visited while in England were small and poor. In one, the church did not even have an office for the pastor, who worked out of his house. Even small churches in this new country had secretaries, and to me this seemed an extravagance.

A Different Side of the U.S.

A few days later, Phil and Julie recommended what they thought was a wonderful idea to introduce me firsthand to the realities of American life. They suggested I spend the summer with a high-spirited group of Christians who traveled the United States holding tent revivals. This seemed a very unusual and interesting thing to do for a proper English lad. I packed my suitcase and met with a group of other believers from the Orlando area who were planning to spend their summer in the same way.

We arrived in Anderson, South Carolina, at about one o'clock in the morning while everyone was asleep—in tents.

This was my introduction to a new way of living. We had long Bible studies in the morning and ate peanut butter and jelly sandwiches, or whatever else was available, for lunch. As a result, to this day I cannot stand peanut butter! In the afternoons, most of us went street witnessing. Following that, we returned to camp, took showers, and had about an hour's free time before participating in long evening revival services. We didn't eat supper until after the evening evangelistic meeting, and by that time, we were pretty much starving.

In this thing as well, I can now see how the Lord was forming me for my ministry to the needy, which was still some years on the horizon. While in England, I truly never knew what it was like to be poor. I had everything I physically needed. While I might not have enjoyed every aspect of my upbringing, my experience was still one sought after and envied by many.

England has what is known as council housing. Here in the United States, the equivalent would be the projects. Back in the sixties and seventies, most of this type of housing was painted a uniformly drab gray. My image of poor people—and their needs, hopes, and problems—was shaped by listening to my mother make derogatory comments about them. She felt these individuals ended up in project-style housing because of some deficiency in their personality and motivation. She believed, as many did, that the poor could have something better if they only tried harder. The Lord had to straighten out my thinking by leading me gradually into his chosen calling for me. Talk about a strange type of work for God to choose for me. I really cannot think of any more unlikely person to minister to the needs of the poor than I. My background completely prejudiced me against it.

The Lord did many wonderful things for me my first summer in the United States, especially by giving me many opportunities to share his Word. Many of the circumstances surrounding those events were quite humorous. For example, the evangelist in charge of the young people that first summer was constantly being asked by one visitor to have me preach. After honoring the request a few times, he said to the lady, "You must sure like what Jeremy has to say."

"Oh, no," she responded. "I don't understand a word of what he says. I just like his British accent!"

God continued showing me the wonders of his provision by supplying my personal needs as well as those of the group.

At the end of the summer, I returned to Orlando and was invited by Phil and Julie to stay with them again. Unfortunately, plans for attending the Bible college in Lakeland did not work out, and I really did not know what I was going to do. A few weeks after returning to Orlando, I met Sylvia, my wife-to-be, and we started dating in September of 1978.

I didn't have any money, so we didn't really go out on dates; it was more like a "hanging out" situation. At twenty-one years old, I was still very immature. Sylvia had been married previously and had a child. At the time, she was working full-time in a daycare center. I was scarcely on my own and did not have any idea how to support myself, let alone a wife and a family. Nevertheless, a few months later, we were married on April 14, 1979. Sylvia paid for everything, even the rings, because I still could not legally work.

Reality hit me like a hammer following the honeymoon. I was anxious to be in full-time ministry, but I failed to see the Lord's dealings in my life. I was leaning on my own understanding and ability, instead of relying on God. Obviously, he knew the significant step I had taken by getting married, and he still had more to teach me. I had also neglected to consider that there could be a significant time difference between receiving the call of God into ministry and being involved in actual ministry.

The biblical example of this is when the shepherd David was called to be king of Israel (1 Sam. 16). Although the prophet Samuel anointed him, it was not until sometime after that he actually took on the role of king. The waiting time did not invalidate God's calling; it was just God's way of doing things, because there is much to be learned in the waiting.

Those in tune with what the Holy Spirit is saying to them hold that word—that call—in their hearts and know they have special purposes set aside for them to perform in the future. Unfortunately, I was not in harmony with God's timing and wanted to be "God's little helper" and for him to move along a bit faster! I thought I could help God out by not waiting for his timing. Consequently, I caused a lot of grief for myself and everyone around me.

One of the first things I did after marrying Sylvia was apply for my green card, which I subsequently obtained. This meant I could now work. The only problem was I was not trained to do anything in particular. I worked a variety of odd jobs and took some community college courses, all the time wanting to be in full-time ministry. The last thing I wanted to do was wait.

I very foolishly launched myself into a full-time volunteer ministry position. A lack of income resulted in our family becoming homeless in late 1981. A kind family in central Florida agreed to shelter Sylvia, our eight-year-old son, Ben, and our two-and-a-half-year-old son, Joshua. Because of my arrogant attitude, that offer did not extend to me.

On the Road

With my wife and family safe and being provided for, I set out on the road. I had enough money for a bus ticket to Dallas, and from then on my mode of transportation was hitchhiking. On a late, cold evening in January of 1982, I arrived in Dallas with about ten dollars in my pocket. I carried a small suitcase, which seemed unbearably heavy. My thumb had been sticking out in the wind for so long it got frozen and sore and felt as if it would drop off.

Just when I was about to give up, an elderly couple stopped their car and asked where I was headed. It turned out they were Christians who actually lived their faith. To me they were like angels sent from heaven. They taught me some incredible lessons. They took me to their home, fed me a delicious meal, gave me a comfortable bed, and took me back to the highway in the morning. Even though it was a dangerous thing for them to do, for me it was a great blessing.

I have found that trials often follow blessings. By the next evening, I had gotten to the New Mexico-Texas border, where I stood out in the blazing sun for hours.

As hard as the lessons were to learn, my homeless experiences helped shape the ministry of Joy Junction. For example, I insist we provide transportation to pick up new residents. I have also instructed my staff to see that guests who come in after the normal arrival time are fed something, no matter what time of the day or night it is.

While I definitely did not enjoy my experience of hunger and homelessness, I know that if I had not gone through it, I would not have appreciated how good a bologna sandwich could taste when you have not eaten for a long time. If that church had not offered me shelter five miles away, I would not have understood how hopelessly distant and unreachable five miles sounds when you are broke, exhausted, and homeless.

Later, I arrived in Phoenix, and friends bought me a bus ticket to Flagstaff where they picked me up and took me to their home in Cameron, Arizona. For the next few weeks, I stayed in Cameron, a little village on an Indian reservation about fifty miles north of Flagstaff. I spent a lot of time thinking about my life's direction.

A few weeks later, on a wing and a prayer—really more of a wing than a prayer—I traveled to Santa Fe, New Mexico, the site of a bloody prison riot a year or so earlier. I heard the penitentiary was hiring prison guards, and the pay was good. After arriving in Santa Fe on a Saturday evening, I stayed in a hotel and the following morning made my way to Christian Life Fellowship, at that time pastored by Carl Conley. He not only became my pastor, but also remained a good friend throughout the years. All these years later, he still maintains an active ministry schedule and travels all over the world.

Another fortuitous event was about to happen. Following the service, a church member offered me a place to stay for a week. Afterward I stayed in the basement of another church member, a local property owner named Rudy Rodriguez. Rudy put me to work painting apartments for him, which must have required continual faith and patience on his part, as I ended up spilling more paint on the floors than I put on the walls. Consequently, even long-suffering Rudy decided it would be best if I looked for another job.

A local hotel hired me, and I worked there for a while, washing dishes and driving their van. During this time, Rudy and the members of the Santa Fe chapter of the Full Gospel Businessmen's Fellowship collected money for me to bring Sylvia and our boys from Florida to Santa Fe. By this time, she was about eight months pregnant.

Sylvia arrived a few weeks later. New Mexico provided a big climate change and a culture shock after living in Florida. While it was good having a job and a roof over our heads, it was not easy living on minimum wage in Santa Fe. Still, we were more blessed than many Americans. Thirty-plus years later, Rudy still helps us. What a blessing he is.

Food for Thought

If all we have done is for ourselves alone, what we have accomplished dies with us. What we have done for others and the world remains.

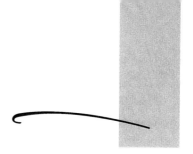

FALTERING FIRST STEPS

Change was in the air again. My boss came to me one day and said that the owner of the hotel had just paid a visit and had decided to make some staff reductions. I was one of those included in the reduction. Sylvia was less than thrilled when I arrived home and told her that I had been laid off. No job meant no money, and that could mean being homeless again.

Before the layoff, however, one of the managers approached me and said he thought it was a blessing that I had lost my job. Seeing my look of amazement, he explained that he felt the Lord was opening the way for me to go into full-time ministry. I was not really enthusiastic about this, thinking how easy it was for him to say this to me since he was still employed. I had a growing family, including a brand-new baby, and no job.

Still, I quickly began reflecting about God's call on my life and wondered if this was indeed the time for me to go into full-time service for the Lord. *But with what?* Definitely not my good looks! I started thinking about a coffeehouse-type of ministry where I could preach the gospel. I started looking for a building.

While walking around Santa Fe one day, I ended up in an older section of town on Agua Fria. I found a strip mall composed of three bright pink buildings. One was a barbershop, and the second was a doctor's office. The store that interested me the most, however, was closed and dark and had windows with holes stuffed full of newspapers to fill the cracks.

I went into the barbershop to see what I could find out. The barber told me that while the empty building was rented, it was only used a couple of days a week. The barber gave me the tenant's phone number.

The next week, I went with Pastor Carl Conley to meet this individual, who ran some sort of a private club on weekends. He agreed to sublet to us, and, thinking he was being very helpful, he said that if the project did not work out, it was all right; we could stop leasing any time we wanted. While I was appreciative of the man's kindness, there was no question in my mind that it would work. It had to.

His Place started as a coffeehouse, at first open only a few hours each evening. I did not really know at that time the specifics of what would occur there, other than that I wanted to tell people about Jesus.

My prayer was quickly granted, but not quite in the way I had envisioned. One night I sat alone in His Place for hours before anyone came by. At about nine thirty at night, a truck stopped by, and I heard some men saying to someone outside, "Go in there. You're wasted. Get some coffee and sober up before you go home to the old lady." For the next couple of hours, I had a captive, albeit drunk, audience to tell about Jesus.

My work at the coffeehouse gave me a taste for ministry, and I began enjoying it. We had potluck suppers every Tuesday, and for a while, it was almost as if we were the only Christian revival center in Santa Fe. When word spread we were giving away free food, that was all she wrote, and the poor, needy, and homeless started coming in. I didn't go out to try and find them—they just found me. Tragically, though, as fast as the homeless started appearing, the Christians who had been coming for the teaching and music ministry started leaving.

As the months sped by, I decided I would really like to turn His Place into an overnight shelter. But there was a problem. With the main tenant occupying the facility for a couple of evenings a week, it just was not possible. So I prayed, asked for the Lord's help, and for once in my life, left things in his hands.

A Learning Time

When the main tenant moved, we eventually opened up as an overnight shelter, offering beds to homeless men. Back in those days, I was still very naive in thinking that if you gave homeless people a place to stay and a meal, they would automatically be grateful. It never occurred to me that people might not be thankful for something free, and that they might even take advantage of you. But my first phone bill showed that there were some homeless people who would not think twice about using you. That was my crash course in running a shelter.

As the months and years went on, His Place gradually assumed more and more responsibility for taking care of Santa Fe's homeless. The daily *Santa Fe New Mexican* published a wonderfully descriptive article about the shelter written in the mid-1980s by freelance writer Douglas Conwell.

> The aim of His Place Coffeehouse is more than physical fare. It also includes spiritual fare. The "His" is Jesus, and the message is that "He" can change lives and give hope to the lost and forlorn. Today, the bright pink building on Agua Fria Street is more than a coffeehouse, although that is how it got its start in July 1982. Now it is a residential shelter for eight men, with a companion women's residence nearby—one of the few resources of its kind in northern New Mexico.
>
> His Place was the idea of a transplanted Englishman named Jeremy Reynalds, who heard the "call of the Lord" to come to America. Reynalds arrived in Orlando, Florida, in 1978, with $50 in his pocket and a sense of mission in his heart. He worked a number of odd jobs,

married, and then moved in with his wife, just cruising about looking for some place to happen.

It happened in Santa Fe, where he was offered a place to live and found employment. It didn't take him long to recognize a "desperate need" for services to the homeless; but he also recognized that as a relative newcomer, there was also a need to establish his own credibility.

Within a short six months, however, Reynalds was serving the ministry of his church, Christian Life Fellowship, through the ministry of the coffeehouse. Reynalds credits the help of several people, including Blackie Gonzales, president of KCHF-TV in Santa Fe, and owner of KDAZ Radio in Albuquerque. Gonzales offered Reynalds half a day's free air time on radio and all the income he could earn from selling advertising spots. Enthusiastic conviction made him a successful salesman. Meanwhile, moral (and later financial) support came from Pastor Carl Conley of Christian Life Fellowship.

First only open for a few hours a day for coffee and doughnuts, His Place remodeled and opened as a shelter for homeless men in November 1983. A similar sized women's residence opened recently. Together, they accept a large number of referrals from police, social services, churches, mental health centers as well as city and state offices. And with at least somewhere for the homeless to go, the possibility of their causing trouble is reduced. As Reynalds said, "Somebody cold and hungry is more likely to steal than somebody well fed."

Not just the homeless come to His Place. There are some area families who are faced with the choice of either eating or paying the rent. They come to His Place so they do not have to make that terrible decision. As Reynalds said, "We help anyone we can in any way we can. We figure if we're going to be in the neighborhood, we'd like to help out."

Being neighborly has been a priority, as some of the nearby residents were not sure about the location of a shelter in their area. Reynalds makes a special effort to communicate and cooperate with these neighbors and keep the area clean and well organized.

His Place does much more than just feed and house people. Of course imparting the message of Jesus Christ is foremost, and residents are required to attend regular devotional services and other events. But religion is seen in context with a person's life in the community and the feeling of self-worth.

Reynalds said that His Place aims to "provide an uplifting atmosphere and to let people know the shelter staff loves and cares for them. Our whole aim is to make people responsible. We help them through a transition from feeling broken down, useless and feeling incapable of feeding themselves or working, to being a person who can put a few bucks away and put a down payment on an apartment."

All residents are expected to find work, but Reynalds tells them, "Hey, I don't expect you to work harder than I do." There is little chance of that—as Reynalds puts in sometimes more than 60 hours a week.

The hundreds who come to the door on Agua Fria have gone through many doors before—doors of divorce, broken homes, alcoholism and drug addiction and aimless wandering from halfway house to rescue mission. Many are in a cycle of poverty, dependent on public assistance that does not meet living expenses but is enough money not to give up. Frequently they have been told they are worthless; and most have come to believe it.

The coffeehouse tries to break that cycle with the force of love, but also with rigidly enforced structure. Each person must search daily for employment. "This is not a flop house," Reynalds emphasized. There are plenty of other places for people to flop.

Although the maximum stay is 14 days, Reynalds is flexible. If someone fails to try and improve their situation, they are asked to leave. On the other hand, if a person is making a genuine effort to succeed and just has not had any luck finding a place to stay, then he or she is allowed to stay longer.

Conwell really captured our reasons for existing, and his article was a great source of encouragement to me. His Place provided a training ground and cemented God's calling on my life to minister to the homeless. But in almost four years of running the shelter, I had taken only four days off. In February of 1986, Sylvia and I took a couple of days rest in Phoenix. During that time, I felt God speaking to me about resigning from my position at His Place, which I did, effective May 31, 1986. Unfortunately, I made a major mistake when I told the Lord I would do whatever he wanted—except that I would never run a shelter again. Never tell the Lord never!

The month of May came very quickly. I looked at the possibility of pastoring a church, but there were no churches available. My replacement for His Place arrived and expected me to be moving on quickly.

The "Almost Homeless" Former Shelter Operator

By this time I was really desperate and needed a place for our family to stay, as our house went with the job. How ironic that the home giver was about to become homeless!

I called a longtime friend who lived in Taos, New Mexico, sixty-five miles north of where we were living, and he offered us a place to stay. The experience tested the friendship of both families, but we all survived the experience, and that friend is now on the board of directors for Joy Junction.

I tried finding employment, but after a few weeks there were still no job offers. I was getting worried and began sinking into depression. While living in Santa Fe, I had made brief contact with an individual running a shelter located on Kirtland Air Force Base. The ministry was called the Reach Out to Jesus Family Chapel, and it was part of a program initiated by the Department of Defense. The program allowed nonprofit corporations to use vacant military buildings to help the homeless. The director of the program invited me to help him.

We stayed for a few weeks, but I knew God had something else for me to do. One morning while praying and considering my future, the Lord called to my mind a vacant property in Albuquerque's South Valley. All I knew about the acreage was that it was large and had formerly been used by an area alcohol and drug rehabilitation program operated by

Christians. It had been vacant for some months following the closure of the program.

I went down one morning to check out the property, and I was impressed with what I saw. I contacted the board president of the group that owned the property and told him I wanted to open a shelter for homeless families, using the available land and buildings. He said he would get back to me. I really was not expecting him or the other board members to take me seriously, but what I didn't know was that prior to my application, several board members had been thinking that a homeless shelter would be a good use for this property. Isn't it amazing how God had given me favor with these men before I even approached them? This is exactly how he works.

A New Home

During the period between His Place and where I was now, God dealt with my heart by showing me in a variety of ways that he still wanted me to house and feed homeless and hungry people. However much I might not have chosen that calling for myself, it was clear this is what God wanted me to do.

A few weeks later, I received a call from the property owners telling me that the board members had accepted my proposal. I was ecstatic! The terms were reasonable, including a week's free rent on a mobile home for my family and five weeks free rent on a ministry building for the homeless. After that, the rent would be $650 a month. While that was not a lot of money, back then it seemed like a fortune. Anything is a great deal when you have next to nothing. But I have always thought the word *poor* can be a relative term. One can be materially poor and spiritually wealthy or vice versa.

In any event, we moved onto the property, which I decided to call Joy Junction. I was extremely grateful we all had a home again. The trailer was not much, but it was home, and we didn't have to share it with anyone. I rapidly became busy. Looking back, I can see several indications God's hand was on the shelter right from the beginning.

First, I began the work because I believed it was God's calling on my life. Second, the timing was right. Shortly after I left the shelter on Kirtland Air Force Base, it closed. A small shelter for families run by another local agency also closed, making Joy Junction the only family shelter in the entire Albuquerque area.

The Joy Junction ministry grew rapidly and so did the income. Shelter income climbed from $11,000 the first year to about $300,000 in 1990. The Lord blessed my efforts, and the shelter quickly gained a good reputation. Joy Junction was often featured in positive stories on local television newscasts and in local newspaper articles. My God-given skill was definitely in the production of publicity to get attention for the ministry.

Although I had previously done everything from keeping the books to teaching many of the regular evening Bible studies, the day-to-day financial management of the shelter began to escape me and those I had entrusted with the accounting. While I knew the shelter was struggling financially, I did not know what to do about it. There were outstanding bills and staff salaries that could not be paid, and I saw no way to get out of the financial hole into which I was all too rapidly sinking.

Crisis!

The pressure quickly mounted, so much so that I felt I just could not take it anymore. I decided the only solution was to go public with the problems the shelter was facing. I announced a public ultimatum that if at least $20,000 was not raised by the end of the next month, I would close Joy Junction. This was not necessarily the best thing to do, but at the time I was absolutely desperate and could not see any other way. I felt totally on my own and did not even know whom to ask for help. Various local television and radio stations publicized the need, and some additional finances started to come in. I thought perhaps things were beginning to look up, but in reality I had not even seen the beginning of where things were headed. A lot of troubles, trials, and trauma lay just a few weeks ahead.

A reporter from the *Albuquerque Journal*, Leah Lorber, called and wanted to do an in-depth story. It became apparent she did not want to do a light, fluffy report detailing the shelter's need, but rather a hard-nosed investigative piece about the problems we were having. It turned out to be the most frightening ordeal of my life.

The next week I spent long hours with Leah. She was going to tell the community why the shelter was in its financial bind, and I was going to be held accountable for everything that had happened. She wanted to see a budget to help explain how we got in such dire financial straits. Now, budgets were foreign to me. I had been so busy raising money to pay bills, answering telephones, signing in homeless people, and running the shelter that the idea of a budget never even occurred to me. Obviously, I had a lot to learn about the financial aspects of running a shelter.

I want to say clearly that while I had the best of intentions, so the road to hell is paved (yes, that old expression is true). And good intentions just do not cut it when you are dealing with the public's money. You have to know what is expected of you. At that point, I honestly did not know. Not even close. I was naive in more ways than one.

The reporter concluded her first session by asking me if I had copies of the shelter's 990, an Internal Revenue Service form that nonprofit organizations are required to submit each year to the IRS. I referred her to the shelter's volunteer bookkeeper, never dreaming what the result might be. A few days later, Leah called me to request a second interview. The questions went something like this: "Jeremy, can you tell me about the bounced checks and the unpaid payroll taxes for the shelter?" My heart sank. How did she know? The volunteer accountant had told her. After all, I never told him he should not, and my sending the reporter to see him made him think he was to answer any question he was asked.

I decided there was only one thing to do. As the reporter continued to reel though a list of problem areas, I looked her right in the eyes and said, "Leah, the public is tired of hearing excuses and seeing the blame put on someone else. As head of Joy Junction, I take the blame. Many of our problems and inefficiencies are due to an excessive workload on my part and an organization that has grown incredibly fast—maybe too fast."

During the next few days, Leah contacted me numerous times and added details to her story. Needless to say, I was growing increasingly apprehensive about exactly how the story would be presented. I rushed to get the newspaper each morning, wondering if that edition of the paper was going to be one where the story would appear.

One Saturday morning, I ran to get the paper and hastily opened it up. The story was worse than I thought. There, right at the top of the main section (above the fold), was a long article headlined "Joy Junction Runs by Seat of the Pants Finances." To add insult to injury, the paper used the worst picture of me I had ever seen.

After letting the article sink in, I dragged myself to the office. The phone started ringing. Some of the callers said they were disgusted and angry. But many calls were supportive. One summed up several others: "You've done too much for too many with too little for too long. It's time we came forward and helped you."

The *Albuquerque Journal* article showed me many things. Some people I believed were real friends completely ignored me after that. Then there were those I never thought even cared for the ministry who came forward and offered prayer and financial support. One of those who stuck with me through everything and encouraged me during this difficult time was Gino Geraci, then an associate pastor of Calvary of Albuquerque and now the pastor of Calvary South Denver. Carl Conley also made himself available to me immediately, as he had for many years, and agreed to step in for as long as I needed him. He also served as board president for a while.

Many people told me afterward that the reason they continued to support the shelter was because I admitted full responsibility. While some of the things for which I was blamed were not directly attributable to me, in a real sense they were, because I was the leader of the ministry.

Months later, when the same reporter interviewed me again, she said she believed me because I had not attempted to hide anything from her. I was open in all my answers to her very probing questions. There was never any hint of financial impropriety or questionable actions. As I said before, the main problem was being overburdened and too busy to oversee everything effectively.

According to Romans 8:28, the Lord turns everything to the good if we let him. The apostle Paul said, "And we know that in all things God works for the good of those who love him, who have been called according to his purpose." That has certainly been proven true in my life and the work of Joy Junction.

The result of Leah's article was the expansion of our ministry board and the Lord's gift of a business manager, something I had needed for a long time. The *Albuquerque Journal* later put it like this: "Joy Junction has bowed to the inevitable and put its financial affairs under the watchful eyes of a business manager." For a while, I joked with our new business manager, calling him "the inevitable."

One vision yet to be fulfilled was the purchase of our fifty-two-acre property in Albuquerque's South Valley. That blessing would come soon enough.

Food for Thought

No matter what your job is, your calling to help others can be fulfilled. Jesus said, "For even the Son of Man did not come to be served, but to serve, and to give his life as a ransom for many" (Mark 10:45).

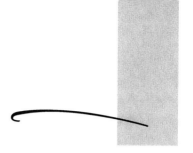

THE PROMISED LAND

The Old Testament tells the story about how the patriarchs traveled through the wilderness to find the Promised Land. From the very beginning of Joy Junction in 1986, the Lord gave me a vision to claim that land in the name of Christ for the homeless of Albuquerque.

Most of the other agencies and ministries in Albuquerque that deal with the homeless are downtown. They have absolutely no room to grow, and even when a possible opportunity presents itself, angry neighbors predictably rise in a chorus of protest against any expansion. We are in a somewhat different situation because Joy Junction's nearest neighbor immediately to the north is the city of Albuquerque's sewage treatment plant.

One day, while speaking to the director of that facility, I told him our two agencies really had a lot in common. A little surprised, he asked why I believed that to be so. I told him, "While everyone is in agreement that we both provide important services for the city, nobody wants either one of us as their next-door neighbor!"

There has been for some time a hostile climate to the homeless in downtown Albuquerque. Proponents of downtown revitalization have felt that for the downtown district to become an area where people want to spend their time, the homeless have to leave. Some years ago, members of a group of individuals and businesses attempting to revamp Albuquerque's jaded downtown image handed out a report filled with recommendations on dealing with the "problem" of the area's homeless population.

Sadly, the homeless were no longer people to be helped—human beings with souls, minds, and bodies. Instead, they were considered a problem that was standing in the way of business and needed to be moved out of the downtown area. No one quite knew where the homeless could be relocated. The only thing the neighborhood association spokespersons could tell the area media was the homeless should not be moved into their area. How deplorable. Tragically, the situation hasn't gotten that much better.

Buying the Land

With this sort of attitude gaining ground in our area, it became important for us to secure our fifty-two-acre property. Let me explain what that entailed. While our landlords had generously offered to donate ten acres to us, we would have to pay the appraised price of $19,000 per acre if we wanted more. We eventually managed to buy the remaining forty-two acres. I am unable to report any dazzling overnight miracles concerning the purchase of this acreage, such as a huge sum of money given to us at the eleventh hour that enabled us to buy the property without going into debt. Rather, it took us a long time to come to the place where we could buy that additional forty-two acres, and the process involved a lot of prayer and a capital campaign of sorts. Fund-raising for capital projects is always difficult, and I pray that this account of how the Lord dealt with us will encourage you.

Having been involved in ministry to the homeless for over thirty years, I have studied quite a lot of material about capital campaigns. Most of what one hears about capital fund drives run by agencies specializing in raising money suggests they are all overwhelmingly successful. Maybe that is because they cost such a huge amount of money to finance. I remember one quote we got from an agency to undertake a capital campaign for Joy Junction was for almost $100,000. This seemed to be a classic case of where, in order to raise money, you had to already have money. Where were we going to get $100,000? My thinking was if we could get ahold of that sort of money, we probably would not need to have a capital campaign in the first place. In any event, not having the money, we mostly went it alone.

With some help from a friend of the shelter, we came up with a nicely-designed appeal letter to our donors, announcing our desire to purchase the property. Despite that letter, on which we pinned all our hopes, we soon realized we had a problem. Although we prayed fervently, money for the capital campaign was not coming in nearly as fast as or in the amount we needed. Therefore, we initially resigned ourselves to settling for the ten free acres our landlords were willing to donate. Of course, I really should have been much more grateful. That ten-acre property donation from our landlords was a great gift and blessing.

Even though the additional funds we needed were not coming in, our landlords (another Christian ministry) told us to be encouraged and said they really believed in what we were doing. They said their donation was prompted by a desire to ensure our successful continuance should we not be able to either raise enough money or convince a bank to give us a loan to secure the rest of the acreage.

We found a Texas-based company that specialized in church bonds to raise money for property acquisition. After reviewing our financial statements, company representatives said they would like to work with us on a program to allow us to buy about twenty-one of the available forty-two acres. A company representative came out to Albuquerque, and we had a series of meetings to try to generate enough interest in the program. After three such meetings, it looked like we had succeeded in our goal.

The Lord, however, who always has an incredible plan as well as a wonderful sense of humor, had something else in mind. I am unable to tell the story any better than *Albuquerque Journal* reporter Paul Logan in a September 1996 story. Here is his account:

> Joy Junction has scrapped plans to sell $330,000 in general obligation bonds and will use a bank loan to buy the land it leases.
>
> The Albuquerque homeless shelter and Bank of New Mexico have signed a letter of commitment for a 15-year mortgage on the 25-acre property and buildings at 4500 Second Street, shelter executive director Jeremy Reynalds said Friday.
>
> The bank became interested in loaning the money to Joy Junction after learning about the shelter's plan to hold a public bond offering, Reynalds said. Great Nation Investment Corp., a Texas investment-banking firm, had been working with the shelter on the bond deal.
>
> A Great Nation representative contacted Bank of New Mexico about investing in the bond deal, banker Steven Scholl said Friday. The bank decided not to invest, but Scholl said he told the representative the bank was "interested from a loan standpoint."
>
> Great Nation passed along Bank of New Mexico's proposal to the shelter. Joy Junction's board decided last week to take the bank up on its offer instead of selling the bonds, Reynalds said.
>
> "By giving us the tip," he said of Great Nation, "they basically did themselves out of business."
>
> Until Bank of New Mexico's interest, Joy Junction and the Amarillo firm were planning to complete the bond deal, Reynalds said.
>
> Earlier this month, Great Nation held three meetings in Albuquerque to answer prospective investors' questions about the bond offering. Reynalds said that about 38 people made bond inquiries and that it was enough investment interest to go ahead with the bond issuance.

Interestingly, by the time everything had been worked out so we could buy the land, our small, locally-owned Bank of New Mexico had been acquired by one of the nation's then megabanks—which had turned us down for a property acquisition loan a few years before.

At about ten o'clock the night before we were due to sign the final documents on Labor Day of 1998, my pager vibrated. Recognizing our landlord's number on the small screen, my heart sank. Being a pessimist by nature, I immediately began thinking, *Oh, well, I guess we won't buy the property after all. Something's gone wrong. After all, why else would there be a call at that time of night?*

I called the number, and our attorney answered the phone. Rather than telling me the sale was off, he just asked me if it could be postponed a few hours. He and the attorney for our landlords were feverishly working on last-minute paperwork and trying to tie up loose ends. I breathed a big sigh of relief.

I slept restlessly that night, but finally the morning came. The big day had arrived: after more than twelve years of renting property, Joy Junction was going to be a property owner. It was still hard for me to believe. I had prayed and dreamed about this day for so long I had a hard time convincing myself it was really happening.

Later that day, I excitedly met our business manager and our attorney over at the title company. Representatives for our landlords turned up a little later. After a three-hour marathon of signing more documents at one time than I had ever signed before, it was all over. We now owned thirty-one acres of property! That included the ten acres gifted to us by our landlords and the twenty-one we had purchased. During a break in the process, our attorney gravely reminded us we were now legally and morally obligated to make a sizable mortgage payment each month. Even though I knew the Lord was faithful to allow us to make that monthly payment for the next fifteen years, I felt he had entrusted us with an awesome responsibility.

Even though I was thrilled that we now owned thirty-one acres, I still had my heart set on the additional twenty-one acres that were still available. And I felt very strongly that the Lord wanted us to buy that acreage.

More Land

I prayed, went over option after option, and sent lots of press releases to the media detailing my concern. And I pleaded with God to make a way for us to buy this additional land. Yet nothing seemed to be happening. For a while, it seemed to me I was the only one who realized (or cared about) the importance of this additional property purchase. My feeling was unless we purchased the available land quickly, we might never get another opportunity. It would be sold to whoever made an offer, and then, I was convinced, the zoning could be changed to disallow a shelter for the homeless. If someone else bought the property, there would be absolutely no chance of ever seeing the land used for the ministry of Joy Junction.

The bank did not want to lend us any more money. Bank officials indicated they were open to talking more at some time in the future, but we did not have the luxury of waiting that long. Understandably, our landlords felt they needed to sell the property as soon as possible. If we were able to come up with cash or proof that a bank was willing to grant us a loan, they would be happy to sell us the property. But if not, they reminded me, a "for sale" sign would be posted. I kept on praying.

A few days later, a postcard miraculously arrived from a company offering church bonds, much like the company we had dealt with previously. This company specialized in assisting churches, not ministries such as Joy Junction. Yet after telephone calls and submitting some financial documents, I learned this group was willing to help us with a bond issuance large enough for us to pay back the debt on the twenty-one acres we bought in 1998—as well as allow us to buy the twenty-one additional acres.

What pleased me no end was that the company was willing to sell most of the bonds to its own investors. This meant it would not be necessary for us to conduct public meetings to sell these bonds to our donors, something that, I explained to company officials, I was far from enthusiastic about doing. On the surface of things, this seemed like the answer to our prayers, but as our business manager consistently reminded me in our weekly meetings, the fees this company charged for their services were very expensive. Consequently, we decided to continue looking for other avenues of funding while keeping our options open with this company.

Sometime later, while listening to early morning talk radio, I heard an advertisement for a small local bank that had recently opened in Albuquerque. Since small local banks are usually thought of as being much more approachable and open to community needs than the national chains, I gave them a call.

Much to my excitement, bank officials expressed an initial interest and encouraged us to stay in touch. After sending the officials our audits and other financial data, two of the bank's officers came down to visit the property. The visit appeared to go smoothly, and I remained quite optimistic that this institution would be willing to provide sufficient financing for us not only to buy the additional acreage we wanted but also to refinance (at a better rate) the property we had already purchased and financed through the other bank.

Everything went just as planned, with no last-minute disasters or even any hitches. Closing day arrived, and along with our business manager, I found myself back again at the title company, signing lots of documents. Joy Junction was now the proud owner of fifty-two acres of property—and responsible for a $7,400 monthly mortgage payment to the bank.

I was elated, as this acquisition allowed the shelter ministry a sense of permanence and stability that as renters we had never experienced. To me, it also meant an increased hope that, however hostile downtown business owners grew toward the homeless, and however large the homeless population grew in Albuquerque, we would be able, with the Lord's help, to be a part of the solution.

Renovation

Now that we owned the property, our next step was renovation, which we could do only as funds became available. On the fifty-two acres sat a beautiful but dilapidated adobe chapel. It has since been demolished. For a number of reasons, it had fallen into disrepair over the thirteen years Joy Junction occupied the other part of the property. Since we are a faith-based ministry, I felt it was important for us to make a statement about what was most important to us. With that in mind, I thought it would be appropriate to renovate the chapel first. At least those were my plans then. How our plans do change!

Let me tell you how the chapel came to be in such a neglected state. I woke up one morning in early 1987 and discovered the entire chapel basement, which was about six feet high, was flooded. The property owners at the time bought a water pump and pumped out the basement, but mixing water with adobe can quickly result in disaster. The chapel was no exception, and that flood nearly became the straw that broke the camel's back. The building already suffered from structural problems, and the water damage, combined with the lack of use, eventually reduced it to a shadow of its former self. But help was on the way in the form of Robert Crawford, a former Joy Junction chaplain.

One day, shortly after buying the first twenty-one acres of our property, I was discussing with one of my staff members what we could do to draw attention to the sad plight of the chapel. Without ever thinking he would agree, we came up with the idea of asking our chaplain if he would consider living on the roof of the chapel for a while. To our amazement, he agreed! We sent out press releases describing the plan. That was the beginning of a torrent of publicity documenting Robert Crawford's forty-day-plus rooftop spiritual experience.

What was interesting to me was this was not the first time I had attempted bringing the plight of the chapel to the attention of the media, but it was the first time I had personalized it. A few weeks prior to this, I had sent a release to Albuquerque media outlets describing the sad condition of a "possibly historic" building. One local television station had responded, but that was it. Nobody else appeared to be interested. But what a difference we saw when we put a living, breathing person on the chapel roof! Here is what one reporter wrote in the *Albuquerque Journal*:

> On the grounds of Joy Junction, Albuquerque's largest emergency homeless shelter, sits the former, and now derelict, Our Lady of Lourdes Chapel. In an attempt to raise public awareness about the need for restoration of this once beautiful building, Joy Junction Chaplain Robert Crawford is forsaking a warm bed and the comforts of home to live on the chapel roof. With Crawford's "home away-from home," a tent, already in place, and a "port-a-john" at the base of the chapel (insurance regulations prevented the "port-a-john" from being hoisted onto the roof), Crawford has begun his adventure.
>
> Shelter director Jeremy Reynalds said he admires Crawford's commitment to seeing the chapel renovated. "Judging from comments I've heard here and there over the past decade, this chapel holds a lot of memories for quite a number of people. It's a beautiful building, possibly historically significant, and we'd like to see it restored to its former beauty. It would be a wonderful place to have services for our guests and also to hold some of our community events," said Reynalds.
>
> Reynalds said that Crawford has told him that he plans to stay on the roof until enough funds have been raised for restoration.
>
> "And that—very conservatively speaking—will be at least $100,000, and that's with a lot of volunteer labor," Reynalds added.
>
> In addition to funds for the chapel renovation, Reynalds said that Crawford is open to donations of home cooked meals, hot cocoa and anything to help pass his time of "exile."
>
> Crawford's wife has declined an offer by her husband to join him in this exciting adventure, saying that there'll be no fighting over the television remote while she and her husband are apart.

The media attention continued. In addition to coverage in the *Journal*, Crawford soon became quite familiar with reporters and photographers from the local CBS, ABC, and NBC affiliates. I am sure they provided some welcome relief from the monotony he experienced while spending so many hours, days, and weeks away from his wife and the comforts of home.

Although Crawford planned to stay on the chapel roof until all the necessary funds were raised to renovate the chapel, the Lord had other plans. He cut short his ambitious plans because he had to leave Joy Junction to go to Missouri and help care for his ailing father. By the end of his rooftop stay, he had raised about $11,000.

Even though we raised only 10 percent of our total goal, the project was not a failure. While I was admittedly disappointed about not reaching the $100,000 mark, I look back at the project as a success—just not the sort of success I had originally envisioned. Why? Because we were able to bring the need of the chapel's restoration to a large number of Albuquerqueans, and out of the efforts of the "rooftop reverend," we had for a while some excellent help in restoring the Our Lady of Lourdes Chapel. Alas, community interest and funding waned, leaving the restoration unfinished. We were, however, able to gather enough interest to do some structural work to keep the chapel from incurring any further damage.

Education for Excellence

My vision for reaching the homeless led to obtaining a bachelor's degree with a focus in journalism and a master's degree in communication from the University of New Mexico. In 2006, after seven years of additional study, I earned a Ph.D. in intercultural education from Biola University in California. The thought of obtaining an undergraduate degree, let alone graduate degrees, was the furthest thing from my mind when I began Joy Junction. After all, I was thirty-three when I began undergraduate studies at UNM, and I had a time-consuming position as director of Joy Junction. Beyond that, I had a wife and five children to care for. Yet I definitely felt the Lord wanted me to refine my skills to do the best possible job for him, and so I embarked on university studies.

I obtained my undergraduate degree in 1996 and a master's degree in 1998. By this time, I was hooked on school and wanted to continue. But a desire to study in a Ph.D. program doesn't always mean you will be able to do so. I was therefore thrilled when I was accepted into the doctoral program in intercultural education at Biola University, located just outside Los Angeles. Although I was busy directing the daily operations at the New Mexico-based ministry of Joy Junction, I also felt God wanted me at Biola. My only option was to commute. One day a week, I flew out to southern California to attend classes.

Feeling this was probably not how the typical shelter director spends his or her time, I thought the local media might be interested in featuring a story on my travels. Consequently, I sent them the following press release:

Joy Junction Founder and Executive Director Jeremy Reynalds is planning on racking up a lot of frequent flyer miles over the next few years. Reynalds has begun taking classes toward his Ph.D. in intercultural education—at Biola University in Southern California. He's flying to Los Angeles every Thursday afternoon and returning to Albuquerque early Friday morning.

Running New Mexico's largest emergency homeless shelter and doing six hours of classes toward an advanced degree would make some younger folk think twice, but Reynalds has never been one to be put off by a challenge. To finance the cost of four air trips a month to California, Reynalds will be teaching two public speaking classes as a part-time instructor at the University of New Mexico.

Reynalds, 42, who has an undergraduate degree in journalism and a master's degree in communication from the University of New Mexico (in addition to being a published author), says he is looking forward to a new school, even if the schedule threatens to be somewhat punishing. "I'm used to hard work and will be in constant contact with Joy Junction for the few hours I'll be in California. I'm also very excited because my schooling thus far has been of tremendous benefit to the shelter."

This release produced much more attention than I originally anticipated. The *Albuquerque Journal* decided to write a personality profile on me and at the same time try to dispel some rumors started about the shelter and me by a small number of disgruntled former residents. The finished product by *Journal* staff writer Rick Nathanson appeared on Friday, November 12, 1999, and it was headlined with a quote from me: "If hoping to get free news coverage to tell the plight of the homeless is shameless self-promotion, then I stand guilty as charged. In order for us to continue getting funds from the community, our name has to be kept before the public." Appropriately, it concluded with a shelter guest summing up her stay by telling the reporter, "Joy Junction allowed the family to stay together, and that's the most important thing."

From 1999 through 2002, I commuted weekly from Albuquerque to Los Angeles. Believe me, this was some sort of feat for someone desperately afraid of flying! The Lord most definitely has ways of keeping us on our toes. He doesn't want us to be afraid of anything and will deal with us directly in the areas where we are fearful.

The Tide of Time

Two dramatic trips punctuated my weekly trips to Biola, one that touched only my life, and another that touched the whole nation. The first event was the death of my mother in 2000. My wife and then my pastor encouraged me to visit her in late February of 2000, a few weeks before she died. I am so glad I made the trip to England when I did.

I made my way slowly up the stairs to the second floor of the hospital in south England where my mother was a "guest" of the country's nationalized health service in the geriatric unit. As I walked through the ward, I passed a number of elderly people in various states of mental and physical decay.

I had been warned that my mother's health was rapidly deteriorating, but I was still shocked when I saw her. She was sleeping, and her breathing was labored. Her hands were badly swollen, and her once immaculately coiffed hair fell untidily in all the wrong places. My mother was not fully aware of her surroundings or who was present.

There was little I could do except express my love. After a second visit, I returned to New Mexico. The following weekend, a nurse called to say my mother was getting steadily worse and that she probably would not live through the day. What else could we do except pray and commit the situation to the Lord? Later, the nurse called again to say Mum had passed on a couple of hours before. I believe one day I will join her around the throne of God, and we will praise and worship him together for all eternity.

The second dramatic event was the tragedy that touched the whole nation on September 11, 2001. I spent September 10 at Biola and was at the Los Angeles Airport early on September 11, expecting to board my regularly scheduled plane back to Albuquerque, as I had each week for a couple of years. I intended to put in a full day's work at the office once I arrived back home. My plans changed that day, as did the lives of millions. Since all planes were grounded, I rented a car and began the long drive back to Albuquerque.

During the journey I listened to whatever radio stations I could pick up. Listeners seemed glad talk radio was giving them an outlet for a collective chat at the electronic fireside. Not surprisingly, many listeners were angry; at the same time, they shared their disbelief that despite all our sophisticated intelligence-gathering techniques, a tragedy of such cataclysmic proportions could occur in the United States of America.

Over the weeks and months that followed 9/11, we learned of many acts of heroism that occurred on that fateful day and the days following. God's name was mentioned often in previously forbidden public places, and there wasn't a peep heard from the ACLU, Americans United for the Separation of Church and State, or other groups trying to strip all vestiges of Christianity from the public square.

Shortly after the tragic event, I wrote that only eternity will fully reveal what we as a nation learned from that consequential day. Sadly, it appears we haven't learned much. We have returned to our former ways of self-sufficiency and lack of dependence on God. I hope we learn before it is too late that the Savior is the only source of all the blessings we continue to enjoy in this great country of ours.

Struggling with Depression

During my years of doctoral work I struggled with depression. Working on a graduate degree is not an easy thing, and directing a ministry for the homeless on a long-term basis takes an emotional toll. I'm afraid the experience of my depression emerged in some of my writing and even in communications to our donors. At that time, I did not know that one battling depression should tell someone what he is feeling and seek professional help. I did not do that, and in late 2004, I was feeling totally alone, deserted, and abandoned.

I asked myself over and over what the solution was. It seemed as if things were falling to pieces around me, and I was powerless to do anything about it. I felt as if I was coming emotionally unglued and that the weight of the shelter's then entire $1.2-million-dollar annual budget rested on my shoulders. There was the weekly payroll to meet, and late in the week we had nowhere near the funds needed. I visualized the line of people trooping into the office in a couple of days, expecting their paychecks. After all, they had a right to do so. They worked for their money, and it was my responsibility to make sure funds were there to make what they had earned a reality.

To make things worse, our business manager told me in a tense telephone call there were insurance payments and a laundry list of other bills demanding our immediate attention. As if that wasn't enough, I found out that a sizable bequest, on which we had been counting to help us navigate through the stormy financial waters leading to the upcoming season of giving, would not arrive until the end of the year.

As I worried about the financial needs of Joy Junction, I experienced chest pains and dark spirits. I felt emotionally traumatized and unable to think. I would have liked nothing better than to jump in my car and drive and drive and drive—and forget about Joy Junction. I wondered if it would always be like this. Many years ago, a friend in Santa Fe gave me some wise advice that I mostly dismissed at that time. He said running a nonprofit organization always means dealing with money woes. "You'll never have enough money," he told me.

The question now was how many more times I could deal with the ever-increasing financial strain. Because we were a faith-based ministry and not a social service agency, we did not receive money from any branch of the government (and that was the way I wanted to keep it). But it meant when we ran short of funds, we could not go to the city council or another government agency, hat in hand, and ask for a financial bailout.

Some people wondered why we couldn't just cut back and live within our means. We did cut back, and we planned a more conservative budget than we might otherwise have done. But we did not even meet that, so we took emergency steps to deal with decreased revenue. We did not want to be examples of the old adage, "When your outgo exceeds your income, it will be your downfall."

But, as I thought about where we could prune costs and provide fewer services, I also reflected on the prior months, which had been the busiest ever in my then eighteen years of running Joy Junction. On many nights during the height of summer, we had sheltered 200 people, and sometimes many more. This was a sharp increase from other years when even in the depth of winter, with temperatures plummeting to forty degrees and at times even lower, we had only sheltered about 150 people. Unfortunately, the increase did not result in a corresponding increase in income to the shelter. We saw one of the worst summer slumps ever in donations.

While nonprofits locally and nationwide anticipate declines in donations during the summer months, until the events of 9/11 we had things pretty well figured out financially. During the last couple of months of the year we always received more income than we needed to run the shelter. For those months, we put the excess funds into a savings account we could draw from to help get through those traditionally difficult and cash-shy summer months.

In addition, prior to 9/11, we had developed a small group of faithful donors who would give us gifts of stock in the summer to sell as needed. We would apply the funds to meet budget deficits. But the events of 9/11 changed the whole giving cycle, resulting in our generating much less revenue than anticipated to carry into the coming year. On top of this, the crash of the dot-coms very effectively disposed of the formerly disposable funds given to us by generous donors.

The Iraq war served to further compound an already very difficult financial situation. Understandably, people were focused on the Middle East and international events. I understood and supported that different focus while significant international issues were being played out, but local needs continued. Homeless women and families were still in desperate need of a safe place to stay, and while we were glad to be able to provide for those needs, we couldn't do so without community participation.

I issued a plea from the bottom of my heart, not only for Joy Junction, but for all the other rescue missions and faith-based ministries around the nation. More than ever, I said, we needed financial and prayer support from our friends to keep going. We knew that God supplies—there was no question about that—but he also uses his children to do so. The depression I felt did not go away, and I wrote this rather revealing letter to supporters:

> I don't feel a whole lot better about life than I did a couple of weeks ago. While I appreciate some heartfelt messages of prayerful support, lack of money continues to be a major problem at Joy Junction, New Mexico's largest emergency homeless shelter.
>
> As requests for emergency food and shelter have continued in torrents, the funds allowing us to provide those services are just

trickling in. That's resulted in our laying off a number of staff and decreasing the number of hours the shelter van is available to provide emergency pick-up service for women and families on the streets. As you can imagine, these decisions weigh on me increasingly heavily—this year for some reason more so than ever. Maybe it's my upcoming 47th birthday and an impending mid-life crisis, or perhaps the stress is something I should expect as a normal part of running a growing ministry.

While some jobs require people to be temporarily on call 24/7, I feel that I'm permanently emotionally and physically tethered to Joy Junction. Whatever I'm doing or wherever I am, the welfare of the shelter and its guests is always on my mind. Whether it's waking up in the middle of the night wondering how to meet this week's bills, a concern about the welfare of a troubled staff member, or thinking of new and creative ways to share the gospel with our diverse population of homeless guests—Joy Junction is always there.

Now while I know being in that state of mind is not necessarily good, for me it is nonetheless a fact of life. So perhaps you're thinking, "Couldn't he leave Joy Junction? After all, no one is forcing him to stay there!" That's absolutely correct. I founded Joy Junction and remain as its executive director purely because I feel that I am where the Lord wants me to be. With that in mind, I ask for your fervent prayers both for me and this ministry as we continue in our nineteenth year of operation.

It is your prayers that will help determine our survival—or not. Because we are a faith-based ministry and not a social service agency we don't intend to ask the government for funds to bail us out. That leaves us with a couple of options. Either additional money has to come in or we have to make more cutbacks in service and while we'll do that if we have to, the prospect of doing so is very painful.

This was a true expression of my feelings at the time, and I could only pray the Lord would use my words to touch the hearts of our supporters.

Separation and Divorce

In retrospect, I see now it was more than the financial difficulties plaguing Joy Junction causing me to feel depressed. For many years, my wife, Sylvia, and I had been having difficulties in our marriage. There were routine arguments and strained communication resulting, at least in part, from the lack of a shared vision.

The unhappy situation at home made me want to retreat into the peace and security of Joy Junction and my educational pursuits. Yet, the more I retreated, the worse things became. Of course, between Joy Junction and flying back and forth to school, my schedule was very demanding. As my studies progressed, there was more and more reading to do for my Ph.D. For the three months before I took what are called, most appropriately, comprehensive examinations in June of 2002, it seemed all I did was read and try to master the literature in my field. I read in bed, in the office, on the plane, and in the gym. Wherever I was, I read.

All the reading was partly a way of dealing with the painful reality that Sylvia and I were growing apart. While we had long discussions about what, if anything, was left of our relationship, they did not resolve anything and ended with arguments and the feeling we were only hurting each other. For the sake of the shelter, a possible divorce was something I always resisted.

Finally, in November of 2004, we agreed it would be best if I moved out of the ministry-provided house that had been our family home since the late 1980s. I moved into a very modest residence located on our fifty-two acre property—so modest, in fact, it did not have a working stove or microwave. While my new living arrangements were sparse and lonely, they were at least peaceful. Basically, I buried myself in my office.

Although I was going through all the motions of running the shelter, issuing news releases and the like, and trying to make sure the money kept coming in, I lost heart in what I was doing. I had shut down emotionally. I saw our guests as just people, not as hurting hearts and souls desperately needing the love and compassion the Lord wanted to minister to them through me. Who knows how long I could have gone on like that before having an emotional meltdown?

I kept a small number of close friends and colleagues apprised of my situation and asked them to pray for my family and me. I am particularly thankful for the way the administrative team at Joy Junction supported me during those difficult days. I believe it is important for Christians to be there to listen or offer some kind words to those both in the church and outside undergoing separation or divorce. Why do we seem to ignore their pain or even treat them with contempt due to their problems, when they so desperately need our words of comfort and encouragement?

One day in February, a man appeared at my office door. He said, "Mr. Reynalds, I'm sorry, but I need to serve you these," and he apologetically gave me divorce papers. I shouldn't have been surprised. After all, Sylvia and I had been living apart for fifteen months, and any emotional bond we once shared had waned. We would soon add to an already unfortunate statistic of the number of evangelical Christians who have been divorced.

As a community leader and the longtime director of Joy Junction, I was supposed to be stoic and unmovable. During the months of my separation and subsequent divorce, a steady parade of people trickled in and out of my office throughout the day, seeking help with their needs, apparently not recognizing I had needs, too.

While my own marriage sadly had fallen apart, Joy Junction was, and is, all about keeping families together, as well as just loving people and giving them hope. The Lord's prompting helped reawaken me to the needs of the hundreds of people and scores of families pouring through Joy Junction, and I realized the Lord's calling on my life had not changed. Only now, I was no longer shut down. I was completely aware of the needs of the downhearted people around me, and I was focused on doing everything I could to provide for them. Although I was unable to save my own marriage, I understand the mission God initially gave me—to keep families together and minister to them as a cohesive unit—is still the foundation of this ministry.

I began to find myself going through a continuing metamorphosis (or maybe epiphany would be a better word) in my life. I fell in love with the Lord again and with the people he provided to help me. I agonized with Joy Junction guests when they were hurt and rejoiced with them when they had even small victories—like celebrating a month of being drug or alcohol free. A staff member once asked me whether it ever gets any easier seeing the continuous stream of needy, precious humanity flowing through our doors. My honest response was "No, it doesn't get any easier. In fact, it gets harder. If you find yourself able to look at our guests without being touched, and their pain and plight doesn't gnaw at your soul, then it is time to start looking for another job."

The Lord prompted me through a former staff member to begin writing a series of books that tell my story, as well as the stories of broken individuals and their trials, and blog pieces focusing on various areas of homeless advocacy. These coincided with a burning passion to encourage people to quit judging the homeless and writing them off, and instead reach out with the love of Jesus and minister to their deepest needs. I never wanted to be guilty of doing what I heard the main character articulate in the movie *The Book of Eli*: "All those years I'd been carrying that book and reading it every day. I forgot to live by what it said: 'Do more for others more than you'd do for yourself!'"

I also increased our outreach to the local community at local networking events. I am also determined to share the stories of the homeless and Joy Junction wherever there is an open door. I strongly believe that we have a biblical and societal responsibility to reach out to the less fortunate among us, and that means telling their stories whenever we can.

A significant expansion in our ministry occurred in late 2009. Just before Joy Junction's 2009 banquet with country singer Rockie Lynne, we published our inaugural issue of the *Joy Junction Gazette*. We reported our wish for a lunch wagon to "go mobile," to feed those individuals who, for whatever reason, did not want to come inside Joy Junction or any other homeless facility in Albuquerque. A few days later, longtime Joy Junction friend Victor Jury, Summit Electric CEO, e-mailed me and directed me to a link on eBay, where there was a lunch wagon for sale. He asked me if we would like it. I took a look and was thrilled with what I saw. Vic was gracious enough to buy it for us, and he flew me out to West Palm Beach, where the vehicle was located. Along with a fellow Joy Junction staff member, I drove what became the Lifeline of Hope back from Florida.

Through the lunch wagon, we have met and served many wonderful people all over the Albuquerque area. The Lifeline of Hope is a continuing part of my evolving life and spiritual journey.

It is a wonderful experience to see downcast faces take on smiles of delight as they sample a good-sized bowl of chili or soup and receive other essential items, such as personal hygiene articles or blankets that many of us tend to take for granted.

While providing thousands of nourishing meals monthly to those outside the walls of Joy Junction, the ministry back at the shelter is still growing by leaps and bounds. We are feeding at least ten thousand meals per month and providing about nine thousand nights of shelter.

Last year, through the kindness of an anonymous donor, we added an additional mobile feeding unit, and to lengthen the lives of both vehicles, we use each one bi-weekly.

Our Christ in Power Program (CIPP) is active and growing. (More on this program later.) We have a number of graduations each year, which are wonderful occasions. At these ceremonies, we present graduates with certificates of completion and recognize their accomplishments. Graduating from the CIPP is no easy feat, and we want to make it an experience to remember. In addition, we have had a number of baptisms and marriages, which are always very exciting.

What breaks my heart and the hearts of our staff members is when our facility is filled to capacity and we have to turn away people who have no other place to go. We know there is a good chance when we say we are full that these precious souls will have to spend the night on the streets. How can anyone possibly get a restful night's sleep on the ever-increasingly dangerous streets of Albuquerque? At the very least, they would have to sleep with one eye open. With that in mind, we are launching expansion and renovation plans at our South Valley property (more on that later) that will help take care of some of the growing number of people seeking help from us in this difficult economy.

What a ride the last thirty years have been at Joy Junction! I am sure, as I continue trusting the Lord, the next thirty and beyond will be even more exciting. I have no plans to retire. When the Lord gives someone a burden to care for hurting people of any kind, that burden must be acted upon. I hope sharing my experiences will help transform a calling into a reality for some of my readers.

Food for Thought

"If you belong to Christ, then you are Abraham's seed and heirs according to the promise" (Gal. 3:29). God has a "promised land" for all of us. It could be anything: a new job, a new perspective, a renewing of a marriage, release from sickness, freedom from bondage to an addiction, a new relationship with our children, or even having a part in emergency caring for the desperate among us. What is God's plan for you?

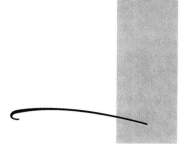

WHEN VISION BECOMES REALITY

W hen Joy Junction started in 1986, I spent long hours on the phone, calling various Albuquerque social service agencies and telling them we would soon be open. This did a couple of very important things. First, the other agencies heard about the opening of the shelter from me and not from someone else. Hearing something directly from the person concerned is one of the best ways to fight off any fear and resulting gossip. Second, it was a way to spread the word around town about our ministry and give other agencies the opportunity to refer guests if they so wished.

Perhaps because of all that time spent on the telephone, a few days before our official opening, Joy Junction welcomed its first family. The man had just been paroled from prison. Along with him were his wife and two children. I was happy. They were delighted. Joy Junction was up and running!

What happened was I had received a call from the adult probation and parole people. Officials there heard about our upcoming opening and wondered if we might be able to take in a family prior to opening day. I agreed on the condition the family indicated a willingness to help out with building cleanup. The parole officer said the only way this gentleman could get out of prison was if he had a place to stay in a shelter like ours. So the family came; soon after, another family called. We had guests and were not even open! What a wonderful way to begin our work.

As time passed I was kept busy answering phones, making sure the evening meal was cooked, and teaching the evening Bible study. Every evening it got very late before I knew it and had not yet thought about going home.

An article by then staff writer David Morrissey appeared in a September 1986 edition of the *Albuquerque Journal* a couple of days after we opened. It was the start of what was to be a very fruitful relationship with all the Albuquerque media. Here is some of it:

> The Friday dedication of the Joy Junction emergency shelter underscores one of Albuquerque's contradictions—in the midst of a citywide housing boom, a growing number of people have no place to live.
>
> The Department of Housing and Urban Development says more than 8,000 housing units were built during the last two years in Albuquerque. Another 2,000 units are now under construction.
>
> There are so many apartments in the city, 15 percent are vacant—a rate twice the national average. At the same time, there are many with no place to call home.
>
> Workers at Albuquerque missions and emergency shelters say the need is growing.
>
> A potluck supper at 6 p.m. Friday will show off one effort to meet the needs of the homeless, said the Rev. Jeremy Reynalds, director of the shelter.
>
> Scheduled to open Oct. 1 [1986], the facility at 4500 2nd St. SW, is located at what was the dormitory of the now-closed Our Lady of Lourdes High School. The building, which is owned by DARE (Drug Alcohol Rehabilitation Enterprises), has been leased to serve as a shelter, said Reynalds.

Joy Junction will provide both emergency and long-term shelter for single women and families, Reynalds said. The need for shelter for these people in Albuquerque is greatest, he added.

Prior to the opening of Joy Junction, which will be able to house a maximum of seven families and 10 women, there were only three emergency shelters in the city with facilities to house families. Those shelters, serving Albuquerque's metropolitan area of more than 400,000 people, could handle a maximum of 14 families.

Joy Junction, a nondenominational ministry, as well as a shelter, will be funded by donations, Reynalds said. It will not seek or accept federal, state, or city funds. The shelter especially needs food and bedding, he said.

Reynalds said he expects the shelter to help out those who are "temporarily economically disadvantaged"—people who can be helped to find new jobs and housing.

"Because of the current economic climate there are people using shelters today who never imagined they would need emergency housing," Reynalds said.

Doing Everything at Once

The first month passed quickly, and sometimes I wondered who and what I was. For the first month or so, I was doing everything. I was the shelter's executive director, but I was also working with private donors and the local food bank to make sure there was always something good to feed those the Lord brought our way. I answered the phone and typed all my own letters. In addition, I prepared the evening Bible studies—and occasionally left to go home to my family.

David Morrissey wrote another piece about Joy Junction on November 27, 1986, a few months after we opened. This time the article profiled one of the first families helped by our shelter. Here is what he wrote:

Pilgrims at the first Thanksgiving gratefully thanked God for bringing them through a difficult and uncertain year.

Ted and Judy Kotoff will offer much the same prayer as they sit down today for their Thanksgiving dinner in Albuquerque.

The Kotoffs, both 32, are in many ways a typical family. They work hard, try to save their money and want the best for their four-year-old son Jesse.

Thanksgiving is a day they reflect on their blessings. But this year Ted and Judy Kotoff are homeless.

Their Thanksgiving table is at Joy Junction, an Albuquerque shelter for homeless families and single women, where they now live in one small bedroom.

They arrived in Albuquerque three weeks ago from South Carolina. They lived in a trailer there—sometimes employed, sometimes looking for work. When jobs proved scarce, they headed west.

It was not so much they intended to stop in Albuquerque, Ted Kotoff explained. It was just that here their meager savings ran out.

By chance they heard of Joy Junction, a shelter in the dormitory of the now-closed Our Lady of Lourdes High School at 4500 Second SW, run by the Rev. Jeremy Reynalds.

"We called Jeremy and he took us in," said Ted. "It's been like an oasis in the storm."

"We're both painters," said Judy Kotoff, adding that she was also an electronics technician while Ted had worked as a mechanic and a musician. "We want to work. We're not afraid of hard work." They followed the construction jobs in South Carolina and other states, trying to make enough to settle down, Ted said. But work was infrequent. Stories of high-paying jobs the next state over proved to be wistful thinking.

When construction went bust, the Kotoffs got on with a carnival in South Carolina, operating rides. But when the carnival operator failed to pay them wages they thought they had earned, they decided to make a new start.

In Albuquerque they found temporary jobs as telephone solicitors, earning $4 an hour, 20 hours a week. While staying at Joy Junction, they hope to save enough for an apartment, and find better-paying jobs.

While the homeless are difficult to count and categorize, the federal Department of Housing and Urban Development says they fall into three categories: people with chronic alcohol and drug problems, people with personal crises, such as battered women and runaway children, and people who have suffered severe economic setbacks, such as losing a job.

City officials across the nation report an increase in the number of middle-class Americans forced into emergency shelters through job loss or sudden catastrophic expenses.

Many of these new poor "are just like you and me," Reynalds said. "They're not street people, but people temporarily down on their luck."

Ted and Judy Kotoff are thankful today, but they are not satisfied.

If they have their way, the nation's homeless population will be cut by at least one family.

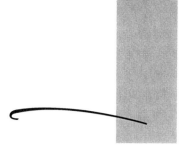

THE HOMELESS SPEAK

Homeless families are the fastest-growing segment of the homeless population. Sadly, shelters that meet the needs of homeless families are not keeping up with the ever-increasing need for their services.

There is no typical homeless family, because all families are made up of different individuals. During my thirty years of running Joy Junction, however, I have seen a number of characteristics common to many homeless families. What follows is a composite picture of a typical homeless family. That means the "Wilson" family does not exist. I have taken many of the most common features I have found in homeless families and woven them into the Wilsons.

A Common Scenario

Let's visit the home of the Wilson family—Robert, Cindy, and their three children. Matthew is seven, Rebecca is five, and JoAnn is two months old. The Wilsons live in Southfield, Michigan, and they have no idea they will soon be living in Albuquerque, New Mexico. In fact, if you asked them where Albuquerque was, they would probably guess it was in Mexico.

It was a worrisome day for Cindy. Only three months before, the plant cut Robert back to twenty-five hours a week, and there were rumors he might be laid off along with one hundred others. Twenty-five-hour paychecks had quickly wreaked havoc with the family budget, so much so that, although it was only eleven in the morning on this particular day, three calls from creditors had already come in, each asking when they could expect payment on long-overdue accounts. Cindy began experiencing that panicky feeling; she was getting overwhelmed. She had no idea what they were going to do.

The door opened, and footsteps along the hallway interrupted her thoughts.

"Robert? What are you...?"

"Honey, I've been laid off."

"Oh no! What are we going to do?"

"I'll file for unemployment and look for another job. I know we'll make it. We've got to. We've got each other."

The next three months flew by. While the unemployment checks kept the wolf away from the door, that was about all they were doing. There were no frills in the Wilson household, just barely enough to pay the rent and the utilities. Robert and Cindy had always paid their bills promptly and had once enjoyed good credit. But that was no more. The creditors continued calling, and the pressures continued mounting. The once free and easy relationship between Robert and Cindy became tense and bitter. Cindy began blaming Robert for the family's financial problems.

One day, Robert was overcome by deep depression. Slumping into his favorite easy chair, drinking a beer and other stronger beverages, he turned on the television. The phone rang, and Cindy answered.

"Robert or Cindy Wilson, please. This is Bill from the NCI Mortgage Company."

"This is Cindy."

"Cindy, we know you're going through a hard time, but we are a bank and not a welfare agency. Unless you can come up with two of your three outstanding mortgage payments, we'll be forced to foreclose in thirty days. I'm sorry."

Cindy hung up the phone in a daze and rushed back into the living room, where Robert was still sprawled before the television. She spewed out a flood of words she really didn't mean.

"Robert, how can you sit there, slugging down beer this early in the morning, when we're about to become homeless? If you really loved me and the kids, you would be out there looking for work. Why haven't you found a job yet?"

The torrent of words continued. Robert got up slowly, scowled at Cindy, and left the house, slamming the door behind him. He walked angrily down the street, resenting Cindy's words all the way. Why didn't she understand that despite all his attempts to find a job, the work he needed to provide for the family just wasn't there? The economy stank. Sure, he could possibly get a job at a convenience store, but it would pay less than a third of what he had been making at the plant. Why bother? A dark depression began to envelop him. A few minutes later, Robert walked into a local bar and began spending money he didn't have and should not have spent.

Cindy ran to her bedroom, flung herself down on her bed, held the pillow for comfort, and wept bitterly. What had she said?

The hours dragged by with no sign of Robert. At dinner, Rebecca innocently said, "Mommy, where's Daddy? I heard you yelling at him."

"Sweetheart," Cindy could feel her emotions begin to rise, and she struggled to control herself, "he'll be back soon." With each word, she lost more control of her emotions, and her voice rose higher and higher. Rebecca burst into tears and was quickly joined by her brother and sister. Cindy ran to her bedroom, grabbing JoAnn on the way and leaving the other two bewildered and scared children in the kitchen.

At one in the morning, Cindy woke to a crying baby. She comforted JoAnn as best she could and ran to check on the other children. They were huddled on the couch with tear-stained faces—fast asleep. Cindy gently placed her children in their beds and returned to an uneasy sleep. She was awakened two hours later by a sheepish Robert, crawling into bed. She reached for him and managed to say between sobs, "Honey, I'm so sorry." They fell asleep in each other's arms, weeping in the midst of a situation over which they had no control.

Robert and Cindy awoke early after a restless night. They prepared breakfast and sent Matthew to school. Rebecca was still sleeping, and JoAnn was gurgling happily. There was time to talk, drink coffee, and get a head start on the day.

Robert spoke first. "Honey, this just isn't working. I've tried. You know I've tried." He started weeping, and Cindy put her arm around him for comfort.

"We could ask my mom and dad," Cindy said.

"No way!" Robert cried. "They were always against us getting married anyway, and they'd love for us to break up. Anyway, they live in public housing and can't have anyone stay with them for more than a few days." Robert suddenly had an idea. "Honey, a few weeks ago, when I was out with the guys, we were just shooting the breeze, and they said there's welding work in Albuquerque, New Mexico. We could…"

"I'm not going to Mexico," Cindy said.

"No, silly," Robert said. "New Mexico, not Mexico. New Mexico's in the United States, stuck between Arizona and Texas. Let's check into it."

The next few days brought a continued barrage of calls from creditors. Robert and Cindy did not even bother answering the phone anymore. What was the point? There was no money to pay the bills. And then a few days later, they did not have to think about the telephone anymore. It was turned off.

One evening, a friend of Robert's came to visit. The conversation quickly shifted to money—or the lack of it.

"Rob, I know there's work in Albuquerque. Welders are getting paid twenty-five dollars an hour. The housing's cheap, and there's plenty of it. Why don't you guys just pack up and go? What've you got to lose?"

A determined look came over Robert's face. "Man, I can't stand this anymore. Cindy, let's do it."

Cindy suddenly recalled something that filled her with more hope than she had experienced in the last few months. "Honey, one of the girls I graduated with from high school moved to Albuquerque. I haven't heard from her in years, but she lives somewhere close to downtown there. I know we could stay with her."

Over the next few days, the Wilsons sold most of their belongings, packed the rest in the dilapidated family station wagon, and set out for Albuquerque. They left Southfield with $350 in their pockets.

About an hour after they started, the radiator began to boil. A few miles later, there was a loud pop, and the car sputtered to a noisy halt.

Robert got out of the car and groaned. There were two flat tires, the radiator was still boiling, and the tailpipe had fallen off. He gave Cindy the bad news.

"I'd better hitch a ride to the nearest gas station," Robert said wearily. "We didn't allow money for car repairs, though."

Five and a half hours and a tow truck later, the Wilsons were on their way again, $250 poorer. Robert said glumly, "There's no way we'll make it to Albuquerque on the money we have left. But let's fill up the tank, get as far as we can, stop at the cheapest motel we can find, and think."

By nightfall, they had covered another two hundred miles, including a brief stop for bologna, mayonnaise, and bread. After checking into a motel, they talked.

Robert said, "Honey, we'll have to stop along the way. I'll work, and we can stay in the missions."

"Missions!" Cindy said, half-frightened and half-angry. "No way! We're not staying in any missions."

"Honey, we might have to, just for a little while, until we can get a few dollars together," said Robert.

They continued their conversation on how the family could best make their way to Albuquerque.

The following morning, after more bologna sandwiches, the Wilson family was on the road again, with thirty-two dollars and a full tank of gas. Nothing was resolved in the motel room discussion, because nothing could be agreed on. The family expedition lasted three weeks, and there were several arguments on the way. Robert and Cindy said many hurtful things to each other in the heat of the moment, and the scars from those hastily spoken words would take many years to heal.

During their trip, minor needs turned into major nightmares. There was no money to buy diapers, and the car's air conditioner broke. Finally, Robert and Cindy saw the signs on the highway they had been waiting for: Welcome to Albuquerque. They hugged and wept for joy. At last! Their long ordeal, they believed, was over.

"Let's go to Twelfth Street Northwest," Cindy said excitedly, "and we'll find Mary. I know where she lives. Look, I've got the last letter she wrote me, and it says the address right here: 1415 Twelfth Street N.W."

The family made their way to the address with much anticipation, but there was no house or apartment, just a parking lot. After asking around, they found no one who even knew who Mary was. After tears of bitter disappointment and a few inquiries into the Albuquerque job market, Robert was convinced there were no welding jobs currently available. The entire family piled back into the car and cried. The Wilsons just sat there, too tired and drained to do anything other than cry—and wait.

Seven hours later, a police officer asked them if he could help. Hearing their story, he said, "There's only one shelter that will take you at this time of night and let you all stay together, and that's Joy Junction." An hour later, Robert, Cindy, and the children arrived at Joy Junction.

A Family Shelter

Because of the shelter's structure, Joy Junction is able to help many families like the Wilsons by providing shelter and keeping the entire family together during a crisis. Unfortunately, shelters like Joy Junction are still very few and far between. Can you imagine how families like the Wilsons would feel if they had to be split up? What would it do to them? It would separate them when they needed each other's support the most.

I hope you are beginning to understand how important family shelters are and how we, as Christians, are biblically obligated to provide more shelters like this one. I reiterate that what you have just read is a composite. While the Wilsons are a fictional homeless family, I drew from characteristics I have noticed in homeless families over a number of years.

I agree with a recent comment made by CNN anchor Don Lemon, who said, "If someone falls into a hole, you get them out. Then figure out why they fell in." As a caring community, we at least need to make the effort to help the homeless get out of the hole. I routinely hear "bumper sticker solutions" for dealing with the homeless living on the streets. They range from comments such as, "They're lazy," to "They don't want to work," and "Tell them to get a job." Okay, so what if we adopt that philosophy and stop helping? Are those who take that kind of an attitude seriously suggesting we let people go hungry on the streets? If we don't help, who will?

Happily, our kindhearted citizens way outnumber a disgruntled man we saw at the home show. I hope he is never afflicted with any form of illness rendering him unable to work and in need of help. Should that ever happen, I pray someone is there to assist him.

No Easy Fix, but Family's Commitment is Paying Off

There's no easy solution for those walking the road to recovery, and most of our Joy Junction guests didn't end up in their current situations overnight. It usually takes a while for them to get back on their feet again. Sometimes it takes two or three—or even more—attempts.

That's the case with Ricardo, late fifties, and his wife Janet. They have two sons, Joe, 14, and Dave, 10. Both Ricardo and Janet are now members of Joy Junction's Christ in Power life recovery program. Joe and Dave are both in gifted programs in local schools.

Why are Ricardo and Janet back at Joy Junction again? Although Ricardo worked hard his entire life, medical issues currently prevent him from working—and he's now facing surgery. He has suffered from post-traumatic stress disorder (PTSD) from a schoolyard accident when he was about nine, and as is common with PTSD, he was also a drug addict for the past forty years.

Janet is from the Democratic Republic of Congo, and she has applied for permanent residency in the United States. She developed some serious mental health challenges that recently resulted in her having to leave the family for a while.

That took a serious emotional toll on Ricardo, and he was barely making ends meet, with each shift at work being a struggle. A couple of years ago he started using meth again. "Not just a little, but a lot of it—and high grade." That wasn't the only terrible mistake he made. "I let another woman move in with me, and she took me back to my old habits. We spent $13, 000 dollars on drugs and alcohol. It was a disastrous plan. I felt like a total failure to my wife, my boys, and myself."

Ricardo was in constant pain and barely feeding his kids. "Now I had blown $13,000 in 401(k) plan money trying very unsuccessfully to start a new career path. I was broken in body and in spirit."

It got so bad that Ricardo became suicidal. He started preparing his boys for life without daddy. His voice cracking as he struggled to talk, he said, "I was trying to impart as much wisdom as I could to them and tell them that they would be okay if anything ever happened to me. I couldn't be any worse than what I was doing, hanging around with dangerous people and doing dangerous things. Life is simplified and easy when you don't care anymore."

The result for Ricardo was, "a destroyed body and a twisted and bent mind." Yet an early spiritual commitment he made to Jesus was still there. Ricardo said, "Through it all, I had a certainty within me. Jesus loves me; God loves me. I am forgiven my sins by the blood of Christ."

He realized there was a battle raging within him. The Enemy was fighting for his soul. Ricardo said, "Playing John Q. Citizen was an abject failure with not much to show for it. So I thought, perhaps, I should go back. Go back to the street life that I had been so good at, or so it seemed." But there was a tugging at his heart. "I knew God loves me and forgives me. I know the only reason I am not dead or doing life in prison without parole is because God has kept me safe. He has a plan for me. So I realized God's hand at work."

While Ricardo still wasn't quite sure about the future with his wife, he decided to rely on God (instead of himself) and focus on his family. Janet was recuperating in El Paso, and with appropriate medication and the hand of God, she appeared to be getting better. Ricardo drove to El Paso and brought her back to Albuquerque. They arrived back in Albuquerque with no money and nowhere to stay.

A friend offered to help the family for a while, but after a month, they needed somewhere else to stay. Ricardo called me and asked if the family could come back to Joy Junction, and I agreed. After things went well for a while, they were accepted into the shelter's life recovery program.

Ricardo's health issues are now being addressed, and Janet is in ongoing treatment. The kids are doing well. Ricardo and Janet have a daily devotional time together. He says, "Struggles are daily, but they have always been, and they always will be. With the level of commitment Janet and I have to God, we are certain we will win the prize Christ has promised us."

Where would Ricardo and Janet have ended up without Joy Junction? Ricardo answers, "We would have been childless, because the kids would be in foster care or on the streets totally homeless. Without the nurturing and stability offered at Joy Junction, the kids wouldn't be the good young men they are." Janet says, "I would have been dead long ago without Joy Junction. You have helped feed me and keep me alive."

What do the boys think of life at Joy Junction? For Joe, "Being at Joy Junction is kinda cool but challenging in a good way." By "challenging," Joe means, "If someone tries to make fun of me, I use their words against them." Dave, very serious, but expressive and animated, said, "The best thing is the diversity of the people." The worst thing? Joy Junction is so far away from town, it takes an hour to get anywhere.

Ricardo wanted to finish our interview by thanking the donors who keep Joy Junction going. He said, "You have no idea of the miracles that are done at Joy Junction, both small and mind-blowing miracles."

Felicity

As I collected case histories and did my questionnaire, every person I asked said they would not stay in a shelter if they had to be separated from their family. Minnesota-born Felicity was no exception. She said it would be too lonely to be separated from her family, and she just would not do it. If she had to be separated, "I'd sleep when I could and travel when I had to, but no shelter."

Felicity had two years of college and was trained in technical-electric assembly. She was receiving Social Security disability and said she became homeless through a drop in her income. Illness caused her to quit working and start receiving Social Security.

"Through Social Security," Felicity said, "my income dropped to half of what I was bringing in per month. To compensate for the lack of money, I had to move to an apartment that was a lot smaller and cheaper than what I was living in." She still was not making it, so she came to Albuquerque after friends told her there was cheaper housing and an overall lower cost of living than in Minnesota. "So I saved my money and drove here in two days."

"Homelessness is very depressing. I miss my home and my things around me. Just to brush my teeth seems a chore, because I have to dig through everything to get my toothbrush. That is, if there is room at the sink even to get it done. I get angry very easily over little things because I cannot even have a minute to myself. Everyone needs a little space to call their own."

Felicity said that while she had relatives, they could not help her because they were on limited incomes. "They're retired, but maintain their homes, as they're paid for. They can't afford to have one more person to feed."

Michael and Lucy

Michael and Lucy moved from Big Springs, Texas, to Albuquerque because of their elder daughter's health. Michael was a high-school graduate, but Lucy had left school in the tenth grade. They had two daughters. Michael's home state was Texas, and Lucy was a native New Mexican. Michael said he was willing to do "anything possible" in the construction field in order to provide for his family.

About his daughter, Michael said, "We can get more help for her here. She's handicapped with epilepsy, and the doctors in Texas were overmedicating her." Michael and Lucy said their relatives were not in a position to help them out in their plight, and they did not have any friends in Albuquerque.

"Homelessness is depressing," Michael said. "There is no privacy, but thankfully we have a roof over our heads, meals for my kids, and a place to sleep." Asked if he would separate from his family in order to have a place to stay, Michael said he would not. "My girls need both of us, and we need them." Michael and Lucy agreed there was a need for more centers like Joy Junction around the country "because there are a lot of families that need the help and shelter."

Charles and Nancy

Charles and Nancy were also residents at Joy Junction. Charles had a ninth-grade education, and Nancy was a high school graduate. They were from Texas and had no children. Charles said he was trained to do landscaping, sprinkler systems repair, construction, paint and bodywork, and plastering.

Nancy recounted how they became homeless. "My husband lost his job in El Paso because the company went out of business. We lost our apartment through lack of money." She said they stayed with friends for a couple of days, until they made enough money to buy bus tickets to Albuquerque.

"We got in Tuesday and went to the Albuquerque Rescue Mission, and they told us about Joy Junction. We called, and they came and picked us up. The people here are very nice and also very polite and understanding and caring." Nancy explained why they could not get any more help than they did from friends. "I didn't want to stay there, because they were into drugs." Their family in El Paso could not help them, because they were already supporting other children.

The couple came to Albuquerque "to stay and get a good job and start a new life here." Nancy said, "It's scary and horrible to be homeless, because living out in the streets you could trust no one. People are getting mugged in front of the El Paso Rescue Mission and the Salvation Army. We are very thankful for Joy Junction having us here."

Nancy believed there were more job opportunities in Albuquerque than in El Paso, and the couple planned on staying here. "It will take time, but with God's help, we are going to get back on our feet again," they said. She said she believed it was very important that more family shelters be built in the United States to give homeless families with children a safe place to stay.

Food for Thought

The prophet Isaiah (Isa. 6: 8) describes how he heard God calling him and how he answered the Lord: "Then I heard the voice of the Lord saying, 'Whom shall I send? And who will go for us?' And I said, 'Here am I. Send me!'"

If we don't help when we identify a need, who will?

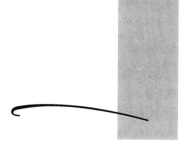

ANGELS IN WORK CLOTHES: MEET SOME OF OUR WORKERS AND HELPERS

From Addict to Chaplain

The media tend to focus on negative issues that routinely surround the homeless. The media understandably focus on this issue because conflict and the unusual are what sell newspapers and draw viewers to the news. But lost in the shuffle are all the homeless people who are quietly making great strides daily toward getting back on their feet again.

Marcos Atwood, now the Joy Junction chaplain, was one of those people. He shared with members of Joy Junction's Christ in Power Life Recovery Program how God changed his life.

Marcos was formerly addicted to cocaine, methamphetamine, marijuana, and alcohol. He's been clean since 2006 and for some time now quietly and unassumingly helping Joy Junction life recovery program participants work through some of the issues they face.

After sharing his story, Marcos said while some participants had known a little about his addiction, others were shocked.

"After class, they told me they feel now that I am able to relate to what they are going through."

Macy and Gina, Formerly Homeless, Now Helpers

When Macy and his family moved from New York to Albuquerque in November 2004, he planned to open his own towing company. Within a year, however, things weren't going too well, and Macy was ready to give up and go back to New York so he could support his family.

God had other plans.

Macy said, "I got down on my knees and prayed to God to help me, to guide me, and give me something that would give my work meaning. Within two weeks I was working with a local nonprofit developing and implementing a vehicle donation program."

After six years, Macy said, this program became the most successful auto donation program for a local nonprofit in New Mexico. In fact, Macy's efforts allowed that nonprofit to earn over $130,000 in just nine months.

"The Lord had given me more than I had ever imagined," Macy said. He subsequently sold his towing business, although he and his wife Gina still work for the new owner, and moved on from that nonprofit.

What would he do next? Macy said his biggest fear in life was that he would become homeless. "It invades my dreams and affects the decisions I make." I wake up at about 2:00 in the morning worrying about being homeless. My heart races and pounds." To help calm down, he wakes up Gina, who brings him back to reality by helping him think how unlikely it would be for the family to become homeless.

Gina told me, "You have no idea how much it affects this man's life."

Macy's grandparents were frequently homeless, going from house to house as a result of his grandfather's alcohol addiction. His mother understandably worried about being homeless, and that passed on to Macy. And his fear has affected his wife Gina. "It's extremely draining, because I have to pull him up constantly out of despair."

Compounding his own fears of homelessness, Macy said it seemed the homeless were constantly around him. He said, "I always saw the homeless here in Albuquerque when driving the tow truck, or when they would ask me at the store for a couple of bucks, or when they would come into my tow yard to buy an old car." Sometimes he would give them money and sometimes not.

He added, "I would put myself in their place, thinking what I would do differently than them. Where would I stay at night and what would I do? Who would help me and my family?"

After leaving the nonprofit, Macy said he thought more than ever about being homeless himself. But there was one positive thought. He said, "I knew about Joy Junction and the good works they do. At least I thought I knew. Once again I needed God's direction in my life and asked him to help me. This is when Joy Junction started to appear to me from everywhere."

Macy became aware of ads for Joy Junction on the radio, TV, in the newspaper, and "even on a lunch truck giving out food down the road from the tow yard. The more I asked the Lord, the more Joy Junction was put in front of me."

Macy said he began finding out all he could about us from the Joy Junction website and from people involved in the nonprofit world. The signs continued.

Late one Saturday afternoon, Macy said, he stopped for a bagel on Albuquerque's East Central, and a homeless woman asked him for some money to get a room, because it was expected to be a cold night. After the exchange, Macy asked if she knew about Joy Junction. The woman said she did, "and she had nothing but praise for Joy Junction," but that it would be full. As a result, Macy said he gave her a few dollars toward the cost of a motel room.

These incidents prompted him and Gina to visit Joy Junction and our thrift store. They were greeted at the guard shack by one of the members of our life recovery program, doing his volunteer assignment. Seeing their Chihuahua, Macy said, led to the man telling them about his dogs. He then shared about how he ended up at Joy Junction.

The man told Macy and Gina how different his life had become "because of the change he received from God and Joy Junction. He spoke to me in such a spirit of thankfulness that I know something good was going on inside this place."

Macy said he and Gina entered the thrift shop and browsed the donated items available for sale. "I immediately thought of the donors who provided this bounty and what part could I do," Macy said. "I knew that there were some old cars and trucks on the property. It looked as if they had been there for a long time. I knew this what was the Lord was trying to show me. I knew this would be my way of helping."

Macy contacted us, and my assistant, Kathy Sotelo, and I gave him a tour. It made a deep impression on him. He said, "I was amazed at what goes on there. From the big common room where three meals a day are provided from their own kitchen, to worship and spiritual guidance, to learning programs, activities, large bathrooms with showers and laundry facilities, and more. There is so much going on there, more than I ever imagined. I wanted to help with this wonderful organization."

And help they have. Our partnership with Macy and his wife means we can now pick up vehicles from all parts of the city, including ones that aren't working or are only good for scrap. It's a great way of turning cars and their dilapidated parts into food for the homeless. It's a win-win for everyone.

(If you live in the Albuquerque area and have a car that's no longer of any use to you, call us at (505) 877 6967. We'll take it off your hands and use it to help continue Joy Junction.)

Harold, a New Life at Sixty-Nine

Another workday dawns for Joy Junction receptionist and dispatcher, Harold Ensor. Like most other workdays, he gets up, makes some coffee, spends time in prayer, watches CNN for a while, checks his e-mail, and then, just before four in the afternoon, heads out the door and over to Joy Junction's front office.

Harold logs on to the computer to begin his workday, which stretches from four to eleven. He says, "The rest of my shift will be a typical workday. I may have some problems, but those are to be expected in any workplace. The bottom line is that I know what this day, tomorrow, and the next day are likely to bring. I have a certainty to my future, and this was not the case sixteen years ago."

In the summer of 1996, on a hot and hazy day, Harold found himself in downtown Albuquerque. He had just gotten off a bus after awakening from a deep, fitful sleep. He said, "I didn't feel all that well. I was looking around when I suddenly realized I did not know where I was or why I was there. Most importantly, I didn't know who I was."

Harold looked around for a while, gazing at what to him were very strange surroundings, and wondered why he was there. He said, "I was thirsty, parched, but I didn't see anything like a water fountain. My hand was putting a cigarette into my mouth. I guessed I smoked."

After talking to a stranger, Harold made his way to the hospital. "I soon realized that the stranger was the first of many strangers I would meet. I would eventually meet family and friends, but my list of strangers got longer, and I still knew no one."

Harold had no ID on him and very little money. "The doctors and nurses huddled, whispered, and glanced at me suspiciously. I didn't blame them. They were questioning what was going on with me, and I was also wondering the same thing. Time occasionally seemed to be in slow motion, and then two or three hours would rush by, and I would still be there, in the bed, literally without a clue."

Harold tried ignoring the fears in the forefront of his thoughts. But they kept rushing in. "My thinking was a jumble of cobwebs, shadows, dark corners, uncertainty, questions, and more questions. I didn't have time to be afraid. Besides, thinking about being afraid was scaring me even more, and I didn't like that."

He didn't know how they did it, but someone found Harold's sister, who lived in Albuquerque. She came to the hospital where they had a very awkward introduction. "I don't know how it was for her, but for me, she was just another strange face among many," Harold said.

"She told me my name was Harold Eansor, and I was fifty years old. She said I drank too much, but that I was an all-around good guy. I tried to be positive and upbeat, saying what I expected others to hear. She seemed genuinely concerned for my welfare, but I was still not going to trust anybody. I felt trust would be a weakness when I needed all the strength I had. I was alone, or so I thought."

Even when Harold looked in the mirror, he didn't see himself—"or this Harold dude." He continued, "It was a strange face. It didn't look like either of us. What was I thinking? I had never seen either of us. The face looked back at me with the same questioning expression that I felt. I felt no recognition, only anger."

In fact, anger overwhelmed Harold. He said he felt angry with himself for not remembering and angry at this Harold in the mirror for not being more forthcoming. He was also angry with those who couldn't tell him what had happened or what he should do. He said, "I chastised myself for feeling this way. I didn't want to alarm the hospital staff with an emotional outburst. They might want to send me to a mental health facility, and I wanted to avoid that."

The hospital had no answers for Harold, but they did make arrangements for him to stay at a men's homeless shelter for a week. His sister wanted to help him but couldn't, as she was downsizing and moving to a much smaller place.

"None of these arrangements bothered me," Harold said, "because I had no expectations, no plans, no goals, and no outlook for tomorrow. Today was about all I could handle, and it was a daunting task indeed." After a week's stay at the Good Shepherd men's shelter, they planned for him to stay at Joy Junction. Harold wasn't thrilled, but that was more a case of him not having any real interest in the plans being made for him. "My only concern was, maybe, where my next pack of cigarettes was coming from, or my next meal, or a change of clothes. I really didn't care about anything else or anyone. I felt guilty about that, but I didn't know what to do about it. I figured I'd let that Harold guy handle it when he got back to the real world, if he ever got back. Where the blazes was he? I wasn't playing with a full deck. Then again, who is? I just didn't care."

Once at Joy Junction, Harold found caring people who were helpful without prying into his situation. "I don't know what else to call it, but my situation seemed to fit the bill, and I felt guarded about my situation."

At the first church service Harold attended at Joy Junction, the visiting minister told the congregation that the Lord had brought each of them there for a reason, and it was up to them to figure out what that was. Harold said, "The cobwebs started to clear. The dark was becoming light. My mind started racing. Hold on—I know Jesus and Jesus knows me. Why had I been thinking I was alone? The Lord was with me. He had been with me, but I had just forgotten for a while. The world around me started to come into focus. I wasn't lost; I was found. I had a future and a purpose. I just needed to figure out exactly what that was."

Joy Junction invited Harold to join the Christ in Power program, and he agreed. The CIPP would give him time to make plans. When Harold graduated the life recovery program, we offered him a staff position. "I accepted and could not have been happier."

Harold has worked in a number of staff positions during the last nineteen years, and he continues to enjoy being part of Joy Junction. "My memory never did come back, but I have had nineteen years to create new memories. Occasionally I have regrets that my memory stayed hidden, but I don't have any misgivings about the last nineteen years."

Harold says his new life has provided him the opportunity to grow as a man and as a disciple of the Lord. He adds, "I have a very close relationship with the Lord, and this has allowed me to continue to progress even when thoughts of my past situation might cause me anguish."

His drinking? Harold stopped drinking alcohol the day he arrived at Joy Junction, and he also quit smoking six years ago. He said, "None of this would have been possible without the strength of the Lord. I asked for some of his strength to help me succeed, and he provided."

While Harold has passed official retirement age, he says he doesn't feel old. "I am able to work, and Joy Junction has asked me to stay on the payroll. I'll admit I'm a little slower getting out of bed in the morning. I probably don't have the stamina I had thirty years ago, but who does? I hope to work until I don't feel like being a part of Joy Junction. With that in mind, I will probably be here for many years to come."

Linus, Finding Meaning in Helping Others

A typical youngster, Linus had it pretty easy growing up in a "big house" right across the street from Albuquerque's Roosevelt Park. His father was a scientist, and after his parents divorced when he was five years old, his mother went to law school and passed the bar exam in 1974. With the exception of first and second grades, Linus attended private schools and received an excellent education.

In high school, Linus played sports and was active in music. Those weren't the only things he tried. With "a very liberal attitude toward drug use and irresponsibility," he began experimenting with what he called "various trendy chemical amusements."

Early on a July 1999 morning came a pounding on his door. It was so loud it was "akin to falling off a cliff," Linus said. "I couldn't find my glasses, but when I answered the door, I could make out the yellow words on blue windbreakers. The words were, 'Victims Assistance Unit.'" What the officers at the door told him would change his life in a dramatic way.

Linus learned a man who was doing odd jobs for his mother, JoAnne, then sixty-one, had attacked her. Media reports said he lived in a shed behind her home. JoAnne had discovered the man had been stealing from her when she found some of her items stashed in his belongings and hidden in her back yard. When the man discovered her going through his possessions, he was so upset he smashed her across the face with a whiskey bottle he had been drinking from. While lying on the ground, Joanne began calling for help. After that, he got on top of her and started smashing her head in with a sledgehammer.

A July 15, 1999 *Albuquerque Journal* report by Jeff Jones said Rex Wilburn Osborne, then forty-one, admitted to hitting JoAnne Carver in the head with a whiskey bottle, choking her into unconsciousness, torching her house, and stealing her minivan. The *Journal* reported, according to a criminal complaint filed against him in Bernalillo County Metro Court, the police also found a bloody sledgehammer at the crime scene.

The blazing house attracted the attention of the fire department. When they arrived, "They discovered my mother barely clinging to life. She was rushed to the hospital where somehow by the grace of God, the doctors managed to save her life. She was comatose, but she was alive."

Linus said his life quickly turned into a whirlwind where time lost meaning. His sisters moved back to Albuquerque in order to care for their mother. Linus said he doesn't know how he or his brother would have coped without their support. Meanwhile, Osborne was caught and put in jail.

The same *Albuquerque Journal* article reported Osborne later allegedly told investigators he had been drinking heavily and smoking crack cocaine the day of the incident. He was sentenced in December of 2000 to thirty-two years in prison.

The weeks flew by for Linus. His mom remained in a coma, and while she eventually woke up, Linus said the family knew she would never fully recover. She was moved to a nursing home. JoAnne didn't much like it there, so one of Linus's sisters (who had moved in with him) would pick her up their mother almost every day and bring her to Linus's house to visit.

For Linus and the family, "those times were good, and we all cherished them very much." But the trauma from the whole incident was very difficult on Linus. "I really descended on the slippery slope of massive drug abuse. Somewhere along the way I just stopped going to work, and when my mother's health took a turn for the worse until she died, I turned even more to the escape the drugs offered. My sister eventually moved out, and I retreated further into depression, rarely going out."

Funds from his mother's estate and the sale of his house enabled Linus to further feed his addiction, and this ran on for some years. Linus said the one good result from his eventual lack of money meant that "I had to drastically cut back on my chemical intake."

Linus drifted for a few years when the money ran out. "I was living in an abandoned shell of a house on some property owned by my sister. I made it through one of Albuquerque's coldest winters there with no heat, electricity, or running water. I was a recluse, but I still managed to get high."

Eventually, his sister sold her property and Linus had to leave. He moved into a friend's spare room for free. "I was making a little money by selling blood plasma, so I would buy food and other stuff like toilet paper. My life was comfortable, but going nowhere."

Linus was regularly surrounded by druggies and drug use, but he declined drugs more often than he accepted them. He wanted to stay away from his former heavy physical addiction. After a while, his friend moved, and Linus said he couldn't go with him. Once again, he had no place to stay.

While thinking about what he was going to do next, Linus ran into his sister unexpectedly at a grocery store and told her about his situation. She agreed to let him stay in her garage as long as he paid her some rent and stopped using drugs. "I said that was very reasonable and moved in that day. I haven't used drugs since."

While this new arrangement gave Linus a roof over his ahead, something was still missing. "I was drifting in a sea of apathy. I only halfheartedly looked for work. Mostly I just stared at the television. I often wondered if there was any purpose in life for me, something that would give it a little meaning. Life drifted by, and I had little to show for it."

When his sister moved to a much smaller place, Linus couldn't go with her. Once again things were up in the air. It was now 2008.

"Looking back," Linus said, "I think God had a plan for me. I had often prayed that I would find something to help me out of my depression and make me feel like a useful person. Little did I know that such a place existed nearby."

That place was Joy Junction Homeless Shelter—a phone call away. Linus said he found the phone book and called Joy Junction. "I got my name on the single male list, and they told me where to be for a pick up." This was a new experience for him. "When I got on the little yellow school bus, I was somewhat nervous, but all the other passengers were friendly, and I soon relaxed a little. When I arrived, they were having Bible study. I stood in the back of the main building, and someone offered me an orange and told me a little bit about how being an overnighter worked. It sounded like a difficult but manageable life."

That was Linus's first Joy Junction experience. "The next morning, after a mostly sleepless night due to the 'snoring bear' on the mat next to me, I helped move linens down to the laundry and set up the tables for breakfast."

After some oatmeal, Linus talked to another shelter guest who told him about CIPP (the Christ in Power Program), our life recovery course. He decided to apply, and a few days later he was accepted as a CIPP participant.

Linus said, "It turned out God was listening to me and gave me what I had been yearning for: a life." He completed the program and graduated. He was then hired as a kitchen staff member where he stayed for some years until moving on to become a driver for our transportation department, and now he is back in the kitchen as manager.

Joy Junction receptionist, Harold Eansor, said Linus has been a great encouragement to him. "Working for Joy Junction is a rewarding experience, but it can have its stressful moments. It's good to have friends at the shelter to talk with and joke with to decompress. Linus is the type to bring a little sunshine into a gloomy room. I am happy to include him on my short list of friends."

A former Joy Junction employee said, "Linus has a heart of gold, truly caring about all around him. He is one of the most compassionate and loving men I have ever met, and his dedication to his work is above and beyond all expectations."

When JoAnne Carver died in 1999, some of her friends told the media that she liked helping the downtrodden. It looks like Linus Carver is keeping her legacy alive.

Diana, Battling RA with a Brand New Attitude

Diana was an addict. Then she found Joy Junction—and Jesus. Today, and with several years of steady employment, she is a different person.

If ten years ago you had asked Diana what lay ahead for her down the road, you would have gotten a pretty vague response. She didn't think she was worth any sort of future—good or bad.

She said, "It wasn't just because I couldn't shake my addiction. It was because I truly believed I was a nobody and a nothing, so why would I have any type of future."

But that has all changed during Diana's time at Joy Junction. She said shelter staff, "saw something in me that I had no clue was there." As a result, her future is bright. "No illness or hard times can make that view change. I have something for my children to be proud of, and to be able to tell their friends when they talk about their mom."

Diana said she has a constant battle with two types of RA—rheumatoid arthritis and a righteous attitude. Considering the pain caused by rheumatoid arthritis, Diana's energy and attitude are amazing. "I get asked things like, 'Why aren't you on disability?' and 'How do you work all the time?' I always have the same answer, 'God.'"

Diana said if it wasn't God's will, then she wouldn't be able to do her job or deal with everything she has to daily. She said, "The days that the pain is so bad . . . I remember I am blessed and that if I don't get up, I may never get up."

While those times are rough for Diana, she said she likes to tell people that while she has "RA," the "RA" she likes to focus on is a righteous attitude. The way her life has evolved over the last few years is proof positive of God's intervention in her life.

As transportation manager for Joy Junction, Diana called what she does "the best job in the world." Her driving position means she is the first contact for a number of our new shelter guests. This is something she holds dear, "because I was them not too long ago. It helps not only to keep me grounded and remind me where I came from, but it lets me help make some of their fears fade away long before we even get back to the property."

Reflecting on her time at Joy Junction, Diana said it has helped make her a productive, strong and loving person. "How many people can say that they have a great support system at work and in their private life? Well, I can. With the things I have gone through with my family and my health, I still stand tall, and I don't stand alone."

Diana is proud of what God has allowed her to accomplish, and she thanks him for all the blessings she has received. "I know without the Lord and my family here at Joy Junction, I would have lost it a very long time ago. But instead of falling into a very deep abyss, I prevail. My 'peeps' have helped me through some of my own trials with their prayers and daily smiles."

Diana has also helped us through some of our trials by making us smile. Thanks, Diana!

Angels with Calculators: Free Tax Preparation from Phil's Tax Services

With tax season and filing time being upon us at time of writing, I wondered how our Joy Junction guests felt about taxes.

After all, while you can never escape from the long arm of the Internal Revenue Service, so to speak, when you're looking for a place to stay and a meal, taxes tend to take a second place, right?

But there are a number of reasons why homeless people should file,[1] even though anyone making an annual income less than $10,150 as a single person or $20,300 as a married person filing jointly is under the threshold for filing taxes[2] and therefore not required to file a tax return.

My staff asked a few of our guests whether they plan to file this year and for those who do file, how much any potential refund they've received helps them out. When confusion about taxes reigns for those of us who do have a job and a stable living situation, it's not surprising that uncertainty about filing was prevalent among those homeless guests to whom we spoke.

One newly homeless guy said he had never filed. He added, "I have heard that if you haven't earned more than $5,000 that you are not able to file taxes. Also the time I did work I never received my W-2 to file taxes. I just don't know how to file taxes or what I would need to file as a homeless person."

We can help him and others at no cost to them. Between February 1 and the end of tax season, Joy Junction is blessed to have Phil's Tax Service twice weekly provide help for our guests.

Shelter case manager, Carl Valles, said the business has been a blessing. "Phil's has great enjoyment and passion providing free tax preparation to the homeless. I also notice their diligence of doing the preparation correctly and following up with residents who were unable to complete their taxes due to missing documents. They also help residents acquire missing paperwork." Valles added, "The residents recognize Phil's Tax Service as friends who provide a most important service to them for free and in a respectful manner."

Another man appreciated his refund, "because the government is helping us from starving. I believe it is a social responsibility of all citizens to care for all other citizens, otherwise it would be chaos." In addition,

---

1   See www.endhomelessness.org/blog/entry/a-few-good-reasons-why-homeless-people-should-do-their-taxes#.VxPJsPkrK71.

2   www.irs.gov/Affordable-Care-Act/Individuals-and-Families/ACA-Individual-Shared-Responsibility-Provision-Calculating-the-Payment.

he added, "It is a way of keeping track of the homeless population and how tax dollars are distributed."

Someone else said he was employed last year and filed taxes. However, he added, "I was unaware of being able to file taxes as a homeless person. Receiving a refund is better than nothing. We should be thankful for what we receive."

Another man said he hasn't filed for five years because he has been unemployed and homeless. He said he tried last year but was told he didn't make enough to file. He added, "And without dependents, you did not get that much back." Weighing heavily on his mind was this thought, "To get your taxes done they charge a lot, and to do it yourself is too complex. I would have to say that I got more (refund) money being homeless here at Joy Junction than we did last year not being homeless. Also, we had our taxes done for free here at Joy Junction."

Someone else said, "Now that I'm in New Mexico I wasn't sure if I was going to file. Phil's Tax Services came here and did it for free, so I filed. I received $54 dollars from federal taxes and was not [required to file] state taxes, because I have not lived in New Mexico [long enough] to qualify.[3]

One woman said while she filed taxes last year, she received a letter from the IRS "stating they need proof that I am who I say I am."

Someone else said she didn't know the tax laws for the homeless.

One poignant comment came from a guy who had been incarcerated for sixteen years. His answer went beyond just the filing of taxes and what he thought about (potential) refunds. "I am new to all these things going on in society. Mentally, I am still institutionalized and unable to understand my freedom and how other people take it for granted. I am just thankful to receive anything at all."

---

3   www.olt.com/main/tc/NM/948.asp.

So, the bottom line for our residents who file is this: You might not get much, but it's a lot when you do not have much.[4]

An Angel Who Makes Residents Feel Safe: Our Security Chief

It's a word more relevant than ever in our increasingly violent culture—*security.*

Conrad Chavira, our chief of security, is an invaluable part of our staff at Joy Junction.

He recently told me about a typical day. His shift is from 3 p.m. till 11 p.m., the busiest time of the day for Joy Junction and most shelters. Once he arrives, Chavira ensures the approximately twenty volunteers assigned to security and the guard shack are in place and performing their duties as they have been trained. A major duty for Chavira is to train these individuals in a job skill, so they have a better chance of obtaining employment when they complete our program.

Another important task is to assist the on-duty resident services supervisor. He helps with inspection of our life recovery program participants' living areas. "With over thirty program living areas on our campus, it can be time consuming. As the shift supervisor inspects for cleanliness and fire hazards, I search for contraband."

Once the living quarters are inspected, it falls to Chavira to check the outer perimeter of our fifty-two acre property, where there are many places to hide from the untrained eye. "I make sure we don't have any squatters camping without our knowledge," Chavira said.

He added, "We have several buildings on property being used for storage and some that are vacant. I conduct security checks to make

---

4   If you employ homeless workers, here's a handy guide: www.eitcoutreach.org/outreach-strategies/homeless/.
And for those of you who just want to know more about filing your taxes, click on this site: http://fox2now.com/2016/04/15/when-are-taxes-due-in-2016-april-18th-6-things -you-should-know/.

sure no one has broken in. I make sure no trespassers are sneaking on to our property."

Chavira said he is a "hands-on" supervisor, and he believes in leading by example. He said his many years of working as a corrections officer at the Penitentiary of New Mexico in Santa Fe paid off for certain aspects of this job.

Always a kind soul, Chavira said dinnertime at Joy Junction is an enjoyable part of his day. "It is wonderful to see so many families enjoy the wonderful food served at Joy Junction. My job is to maintain order while food and drinks are being served. I want to make sure the children are fed and we have enough drinks to go around. The residents know there is no fighting, arguing or running when Conrad's on duty."

When guests arrive on property, they are searched for alcohol and illegal drugs. Weapons are often confiscated as well. Chavira said, "I train the security volunteers on different techniques in searching for contraband."

Chavira also runs a background check on new guests. "When new guests arrive on property, I search their records for any criminal activity that precludes them from staying at Joy Junction. In certain cases, it is my job to advise an unwelcome guest that they must leave and not return. It is very important that I ensure the safety of all our guests and our staff members."

Another part of Chavira's duties as chief of security is to administer urine analysis drug tests to programmers and residents. He gives blood alcohol tests as well. "The sobriety of all our guests is very important to me."

Throughout the evening, Chavira stays busy walking around the grounds making sure none of the shelter guests are loitering in restricted areas. He added, "It is my job to make sure male and female guests are not fraternizing with one another. I make sure the children are close to their parents and no harm comes to them."

Chavira also monitors surveillance cameras. He said, "These cameras are a very important tool in a facility such as ours. I monitor, and on occasions, review activity on the cameras. When purses are stolen or property is misplaced, I am able to review the video feed and conduct investigations."

Chavira's many years of working as a police officer and a private investigator have come in handy.

He has, on occasion, conducted training for staff members, as well, and had put together a policy on how to deal with an "active shooter" situation. He said, "Unfortunately, in this day and age we must be prepared for anyone who tries to harm our guests and staff."

I have occasionally asked Chavira to conduct investigations where staff may be involved. On one occasion, I asked him to return to the property because of what looked on security cameras as if some funny business was taking place in our kitchen. Chavira's actions and professionalism that night helped us solve what we learned had been an ongoing issue.

Chavira also periodically helps our resident service staff. He said, "On several occasions I have been asked to cover for a supervisor on sick leave or on vacation. The supervisor has a very stressful job, and I am always willing to help."

Chavira said he enjoys working at Joy Junction and is proud to be part of the almost three-decade-old ministry. He concluded, "It has changed my life in so many ways and has made me a better person. It is a great feeling at the end of the day to know that I may have helped someone one way or another."

Thanks, Conrad. We appreciate your commitment.

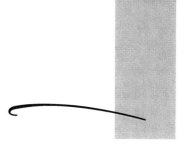

Some People with Surprising Stories

It is tempting to categorize the people who come to Joy Junction or meet on the street as lacking incentive, being lazy, or not wanting to work. Having met many homeless people over the past thirty years, we know that there are many reasons and circumstances leading to loss of a home or a job. Following are some stories that may surprise you.

Mark

It is never easy being homeless, and the difficulties are compounded when one is seventy-five years old. That was the plight faced by Mark, one of our Joy Junction guests and a participant in our life recovery program. Mark was a retired electrician who lives on a small amount of social security money. It is definitely not enough money to make ends meet, especially when battling an alcohol addiction.

Mark was evicted from his apartment because his money went to alcohol instead of paying his rent. "They brought me a notice from their lawyer saying that I had been unruly and arguing with other tenants. I decided not to even worry about it. If they didn't want me in the building, I didn't want to be there, either. That was my attitude."

Mark admitted he had probably been unruly as a result of being intoxicated. Still, he was angry about being homeless. And he was definitely scared. "I have slept outside a few times, but I certainly do not like it out on the streets. It's dangerous."

Mark knew he needed more than just shelter. He had to find a program to help him with his addiction. He was aware of Joy Junction, so a few months ago he began as an overnight guest and was accepted when he applied to join our life recovery program. He said things are usually good for him these days and that he enjoys being around people who are recovering from addiction issues. "I have made friends, and I know some who have done well and actually overcome their addiction. No one can tell what tomorrow will bring us, but I do get hope from that and from the friends I've made here at Joy Junction. I think if they can do that, I can do that, too."

After breaking a hip and a shoulder, Mark has some health problems in addition to his addiction. He says he doesn't really know where he would be without Joy Junction. "I knew of Joy Junction. I had heard of them from my work with the Salvation Army." He added, "I also worked at a mission a long time ago helping others. I like helping other people, but now I'm the one who needs it. I ask for help every night from the Lord, and I get answers."

Being at Joy Junction helped Mark in his fight against alcoholism, but his battle is never easy. "The help I need is in the area of defeating an addiction. You never really defeat it, but in overcoming my addiction, I like being here because I feel strength and faith. I hope that eventually I can leave Joy Junction—but not right at this time."

Without our wonderful donors who give to Joy Junction every month, we could not be here for our guests like Mark. I asked Mark what he would like to tell them. He made it clear he appreciates them very much: "They made it possible for me to have hope and resume faith. I've been a Christian for a while, a long while, but I strayed away. Their donations make this all possible. There is no way I could be here unless Joy Junction was helped by other people. I like our life recovery classes. I like being around the other people who are recovering and who have faith in God and Jesus."

If he had one wish, Mark would "pray for strength that I won't give up, and I don't plan on giving up. I get strength from the other people here, the teachers, and the staff. It makes me very hopeful that there are good things to come."

Please pray for Mark.

Beth, Billie, and Jenny

Joy Junction's faith-based, multi-stage Christ in Power Program (CIPP) revolves around the changes necessary for our guests to get back on their feet. Graduating members of Joy Junction's nine-month life recovery program receive their certificates at a very special ceremony. While some smile, others are very nervous. They all work hard to complete their program, and they all deserve their special moment of recognition.

People come to Joy Junction for many reasons. For some residents, it is the difficult economy and the lack of ability to cope with life in our ever-increasingly stressful society. Others struggle with drugs, alcohol, poor money management, poor parenting skills, and mental health issues.

Three of our graduates told us a little bit about their lives and what being in the program meant to them.

Beth was an abuse and rape victim. Before she came to Joy Junction, she lived with her cousin and tried to find a job. Unable to find employment, she was asked to leave her cousin's apartment and ended up at the shelter. Beth described how she felt on her arrival at Joy Junction. "When I got here, I was nervous and scared, because I didn't know anyone and I was alone."

Although she was alone, she felt safe, and she quickly realized she did not want to leave the security of Joy Junction and deal with the uncertainties and dangers lurking on downtown Albuquerque streets. It didn't take Beth long to realize that joining the CIPP would be the right decision for her.

Although the CIPP was sometimes difficult for her and initially she felt that God wasn't there for her, Beth feels much differently now. Most importantly, she's gotten closer to the Lord and has developed better life skills. She said she knows also if she needs to talk, she can share her heart with our staff as well as directly with the Lord.

She said, "The program has taught me how to handle things better at a job. I also know that everyone here cares and loves me along with God, and that I also have a roof over my head and food to eat. It has helped me to feel safe here."

Beth said she is so happy she finished something she started without having to have someone push her through it. "Thank you, guys, for being there for me and helping me through my problems and the negative things I have gone through most of my life."

Billie also told us her story. Mother to three beautiful children, she and her husband have been at Joy Junction for a little more than a year. Billie came to Joy Junction because she had never had a real job. Her "employment" had been trafficking drugs. After serving her time, an extended stay with relatives didn't work out for the family, and they were eventually forced to leave.

This was not Billie's first stay with us, for she recalled being here when she was nine years old after her mother fled an abusive relationship. She lost her dad due to alcohol when she was eight and had lived on her own since she was fourteen years old. She admitted dabbling with drugs and alcohol even back then, but she said addiction was never a "real" problem.

She did say, though, that she had been "confused" about God for all her life. When she lost her mother, she blamed God and asked why he would make her suffer. After joining the CIPP and graduating seven months later, Billie now has a different perspective. She said not only did she learn about the Lord's love for her, but, very importantly for her recovery and self-esteem, she was also able to finish something she started.

She added, "I know God brought me here to strengthen my relationship with my family and get to know him better. I am very grateful for Joy Junction and what they have taught me. It is not just a homeless shelter; it is more like a family."

Sometimes it takes more than one attempt to successfully complete the CIPP. Jenny first came to Joy Junction with a meth and alcohol addiction. She had also endured and finally left an almost two-decade-long abusive relationship.

Her first time around, Jenny completed about half the CIPP before she left. It wasn't easy for her expanding family. She got pregnant after leaving Joy Junction and, along with her daughter and boyfriend, moved from motel to motel for a while. Eventually, her boyfriend obtained employment, and the family was able to get an apartment just before the birth of her son.

More problems lay ahead. During her pregnancy and the subsequent birth of her son, Jenny was having serious kidney issues, while her boyfriend was having problems with his gallbladder. She had five surgeries on her kidneys, and her boyfriend was also hospitalized. As a result, they ended up behind in their rent and lost their apartment. After this, they came back to Joy Junction and rejoined the program.

Jenny said, "I hadn't finished high school, and I've gone to college a couple of times but never finished anything that I have started. Finally, I finished something—the CIPP. Being on the CIPP and successfully finishing it has brought up my self-esteem, and it makes me feel good to help people."

Jenny has also been clean from her meth addiction for a couple of years, and that, she said, makes her "feel good." As a CIPP graduate, she is continuing for the moment to serve those individuals in similar circumstances to those she was in not so long ago.

She said, "To give back to the community of the homeless is a great honor, and it makes me appreciate everything Joy Junction has taught me and done for me."

George

He didn't know it at the time, but George was about to find out the truth of the Scripture, "Your enemy the devil prowls around like a roaring lion looking for someone to devour" (1 Peter 5:8). Sometimes the Enemy uses those you may least expect, like your coworkers.

George and his family moved to Albuquerque from Reno, Nevada, for a new job in Rio Rancho. Wanting to fit in with his coworkers, George started using crack cocaine and became addicted. After a lot of anguish and turmoil caused by George's drug abuse, he quit his job. Soon, there was no more money. As a result, along with his wife, Colleen, and their three children, George came to Joy Junction.

Hoping to permanently conquer what had become a life-controlling and family-threatening addiction, George joined Joy Junction's life recovery program, the Christ in Power Program. "My wife told me for a long time to get help, and I figured this was the place to get it. While on the CIPP, I learned more about God and myself than I ever could have on my own."

While George had been doing well, he was about to hit a serious bump in the road. "As I was getting better with my addiction and closer to God, I hit a 'self-destruction relapse' button." George relapsed twice, both times leaving Joy Junction property before succumbing to his old addiction. He said, "That caused me to almost lose my family twice."

When he used drugs, he had no idea what he was doing to his family. "My wife and I have three children. I would spend our money and then tell my kids no about going to the store. I would always put them last, but they never put me last. For almost two years, I did this to my family. My wife would even try to hide money."

By God's grace, George worked through his issues. After we saw the progress he was making, we offered him a staff position at Joy Junction. George accepted, and he worked for us and lived on-site for quite a while. When another, higher paying job offer came along, he felt it was time to move on.

Reflecting on that time in his life, George said, "During my stay at Joy Junction, I received a lot of compassion and a desire to develop a closer relationship to God. The staff here taught me a better way to live with God in my life. After I learned to love my family again, I got a better job. I worked for my family, not for me. I put my notice in and went to work at a tire shop."

Excited about their future, George, Colleen, and the kids never dreamed what trials lay ahead. George suffered a massive heart attack. He recalled asking the Lord for his help. After one year of recuperation, he was able to return to work, but he ended up with a hernia and a nine-month recovery period. As a result, the family got behind on their rent and was evicted. That caused their return to Joy Junction.

Surprisingly, George isn't angry about all the ups and downs he's experienced in life. He said his current stay at Joy Junction has been the most rewarding ever for him and his family. "We have more love for God, which reflects on to the other people staying here who want that same experience for themselves. I praise Joy Junction for the reason they're here—not for the symbol of homelessness, but the symbol of love and of the hope of Jesus Christ for all who come here!"

It is such a joy to see George's and Colleen's happy, smiling faces at our church services. It is thrilling to report George has now been drug-free for years, and he has never relapsed. I am also grateful that when George and Colleen had no place to stay, they knew to call Joy Junction. When they are ready and able, we want to see them return to self-sufficiency. Meanwhile, we believe that every day they live and serve the Lord while they stay at Joy Junction is a step in that direction.

Fiona

Since she was a child, Fiona prayed for a baby boy. The Lord fulfilled the desire of Fiona's heart. But, about a month later, the baby's father left. Fiona said he couldn't handle the attention being lavished on his new son, Jack. He did, however, come by weekly to spend about a half hour with his son.

Those visits decreased and then stopped entirely. When Jack was three or four years old, his dad would tell him he would come and pick him up for the weekend. Fiona said, "Jack would get his overnight bag and sit on the curb and wait for his father who would never show up. After a while, he would come in with tears and ask me why, and it would crush my heart." As that same scenario played out over and over, Fiona said resentment and anger followed.

Fiona recalled that when Jack was four, she met a man who was a chef. They started dating, and both Fiona and Jack fell in love with him. Her son's affection, and the fact that the three of them went camping and fishing together, thrilled Fiona. She was delighted that the man she had chosen to be in her life loved her son as his own.

But there was a side to this man that Fiona didn't know, and it didn't surface until they had both gotten a job at a local bar. At first her life with this man was fun and exciting, but it quickly became a nightmare. The man she thought loved her was drunk 24/7. Black eyes and a smashed head became the norm for Fiona.

One night, it was especially bad. "As we were walking, he turned around and pushed me in the chest, and I flew backward. I cracked my head wide open. I heard my son's blood-curdling scream and managed to run to him. I just couldn't imagine what he felt like, seeing my face and clothes drenched in blood. I just held him as he cried."

Fiona left this man, but more trauma was on the horizon. Initially comforting, the trauma took the form of a male friend Fiona had been supporting—until she caught him lying, cheating, and stealing. Although Fiona told him to leave, he began stalking her, making unwanted calls, and even going to her place of employment. Desperate, Fiona moved. That wasn't enough, though, as he still found her. At that point, he started abusing Jack emotionally and Fiona physically.

Fiona recalled a terrifying incident when he broke into her apartment in the middle of the night. He wanted to use the phone. As she had to get up at four, Fiona told him to hurry up. "He threw the phone at me, and it hit me in the temple. All I felt was warm fluid rushing down my face, and I heard my son running into the room. Fed up with me getting hit all the time and abused verbally, emotionally, and physically, he started hitting, screaming, and crying."

On another occasion, this human nightmare again broke into her apartment. He said he wanted to talk to her. Fiona said, "I wanted nothing to do with him. I was so afraid. He grabbed me by my hair, turned me to face him, and punched me in my right eye. To this day, I can't see really well out of it, as it is still a little blurry. My son and another friend spending the night ran into the room, and there it was again, my son angry and terrified."

Although law enforcement was called, nothing came of it. The nightmare continued. "A couple of weeks later, I woke up to pain and about three hundred pounds of pressure on top of me. He had taped plastic gloves on his hands and was ripping me up inside. I came to find out he had raped another woman shortly before. Needless to say, I didn't press charges."

While things settled down for a while, it was too little too late for her son, who, by this time, was a very angry middle-schooler. Unbeknownst to his mother, he had joined a gang. At this point, her little boy was no longer her little boy. He had so much anger and was so out of control, they couldn't talk. Fiona prayed moving to a new house might help Jack.

Although she still had her job at a fast-food restaurant, Fiona said by this time she was a hard alcoholic. "I had whiskey with my beer, come home and relax, and I didn't go anywhere without my son." As the months went on, Fiona said she became close to a man who lived just across the street from her and Jack. Initially, she said, Warren was gentle, kind, caring, and giving. Her son became good friends with him.

Eventually, Warren moved into their home. She remembered, "It was wonderful. The feeling in our home was very warm, and it felt blessed. The only thing that was uncomfortable was he was so jealous of everything and anything." Fiona said she didn't know at first that Warren had a bad cocaine problem. When she found out and they talked about it, he told her he was doing an eight ball a day.

"I went, 'Wow,'" Fiona said. "I couldn't believe it. But it made sense. When he was drinking beer and snorting coke, he would become extremely jealous and intimidating." The situation worsened when Fiona discovered she had about one hundred dollars less cash than she had estimated. She asked Warren what happened with the missing money. His answer was not what she expected. "He slapped me so hard my ear rang. I found myself lying back with his hand around my throat. I could not breathe. For some reason, he stopped. I played it cool to be able to get out."

Fiona walked down the stairs to her neighbor who was cooking breakfast. "I wanted to tell her what was going on. But, of course, I knew he would come and see what was up." Warren did just that, and all Fiona remembers about what happened next is a blur. When she came to, she was in her house, and the paramedics were stumbling around looking for a light switch.

She had received a terrible beating from the man she had been planning on marrying in six days. "I am pretty sure I was in total shock. To this day, I do not remember a thing, and my ear still hurts me badly."

After Fiona's traumatic beating and emergency room trip, Jack told her more of what had happened. It was Jack who called the police. He told her that after the beating, Warren told him, "You better go check on your mom. I think I might have killed her."

And, in fact, it is amazing Fiona is still alive. She attributes that to the grace of God. She said that following the incident, "My son found part of my skull in the kitchen, crime scene and all. No child should have to go through that at any age and for so many years." Thankfully, Warren is no longer a problem to her or Jack.

It was at this point that Fiona and Jack lost contact for a while. They were both on the streets, but not together. Fiona was still drinking heavily, and Jack, understandably angry, was struggling with a gang mentality. Fiona would quite often come into Joy Junction on an overnight basis and leave the next morning.

She said, "Before my son and I came to Joy Junction together, I came alone here and there. I couldn't find him, and he couldn't find me. It was a living nightmare. I would close my eyes and picture him shot or stabbed to death—24/7." Finally, they reestablished contact, and the two of them began coming into Joy Junction together. However, because Fiona and Jack were at that point staying at Joy Junction on a nightly basis, their beds were not guaranteed. On one particularly busy night for Joy Junction, they called in too late.

She said, poignantly, "We ended up behind a McDonald's dumpster downtown. Most of the time, we were together on the streets, scared and hungry. We hustled to get what we needed." It is terrifying to think what could have happened to them. Fiona and Jack disappeared for a while but resurfaced a few months later. A Joy Junction staff member said, "When they came back, Jack had added some pounds and was definitely more grown-up. You could tell, though, that they had been living on the streets."

It wasn't long after this that Fiona asked Jesus into her life. Fiona said, "By God's will, day by day we will get stronger. Jack is my life, and with the Lord Jesus Christ, we now have a life." She is now one of the program members most of the others respect. Watching this transformation in both of them and the resulting changes in the family unit, has been interesting and gratifying.

Thank God he had his mighty hand of protection over Fiona both during and after her awful abuse. I believe the Lord will continue healing the emotional scars with which Fiona and Jack are still dealing. And thank God for allowing us to keep the Joy Junction doors open so we can be there for the many other Fionas and Jacks who are out there on the streets of Albuquerque and need our help.

Marsha

Marsha's long and winding road to Joy Junction began over sixty years ago with a grandfather who sexually abused all the girls in the family.

The abuse had profound effects on Marsha as she grew up. When she went through puberty, acting out with boys and men became a way of life. Marsha got pregnant and initially planned on going to El Paso for an abortion. But her moral code was pro-life, and so she gave the baby up for adoption.

Marsha had strict guidelines for prospective adoptive parents. They had to be Christian and involved with the community and have a military background. "I wanted my child to be safe," she said. "God, I believe, was my strength and salvation in this effort. He put me on a path where my well-intentioned goal was met. Through prayer, he gave me the strength and wisdom to find the right help as well as locate a nice family."

Marsha came to Albuquerque and started working in hotels, something she did for twenty-seven years. She progressed from being a front desk clerk to working as a reservation and sales manager. But Marsha was beginning a downhill emotional slide. "Depression had become a continuing problem, as well as [a] lack of trust in authority figures. I was married for seven years, and depression and anxiety led to divorce. I became increasingly isolated." She thought of ending her life.

After almost three decades of working in hotels, Marsha decided a change was in order when a new company took over the hotel where she worked. She got a new job at a country club. That went well until, after eight years, sexual harassment became an issue, dredging up old, painful, and buried memories. She realized the need to face these issues and began dealing with them. As she did so, the Lord intervened. "That," Marsha said, "helped me to erase part of the past and start to understand God's grace."

Marsha's life took another difficult turn when her mother passed away. "That," she said, "led to more running and a change of jobs." At that point, her son contacted her. She said while there was a honeymoon period, "not all tales are fairy tales." She said, "I do not believe God wanted me involved in his life, long-term. He did, however, want my son to know who I was. But this is when I began to understand the dangers of trying to live up to other people's expectations. I came home again."

Marsha now battled chronic depression. As a result of cuts in mental health services, the assistance she had been relying on was no longer there for her. She ended up homeless and arrived at Joy Junction one day at about four-thirty in the morning. This was her first experience of homelessness, a challenging and sometimes terrifying experience for anyone. Her experience was a good one. "Everyone was very nice and helpful."

When she learned of Joy Junction's CIPP life recovery program, she joined. She thought it could help her successfully face the issues she had battled for so long. With assistance from the shelter and outside medical professionals, Marsha began working on the roots of her depression and anxiety.

She said, "With the power of faith and Jesus as my Savior, I have conquered the persistent depression and running away from pain or hurt. The Lord is still teaching me to stand and accept the blessings and trials he uses to make me strong. I no longer wish to end my life. I feel that God will use me as a tool to glorify him. I can still have my feelings hurt, but the depression is no longer dark and damaging. Joy Junction cared, and through my ups and downs in the program, they have continued to care. I have changed. I am not perfect, but I am continuing to change. I am born again and more joyful in life and thankful for life."

Marsha expects nothing and gives everything. She will tell you what a blessing Joy Junction has been to her, but she has done a lot of blessing of her own, blessing us and many of the people who are in need of our help.

Raymond

While at the Albuquerque Convention Center for our annual pre-Thanksgiving Day feast one year, I just "happened" (I never think of these meetings as coincidences) to be introduced to Raymond. He was there as a volunteer, helping serve hundreds of hungry people. But not so long ago, Raymond was himself homeless and staying at Joy Junction. Here is some of his story.

Formerly homeless on the streets of California, Raymond ended up in Albuquerque and at Joy Junction. As a result of his homelessness and other issues, he was in despair. "I was hopeless when I first got there, and Joy Junction gave me the tools I needed, such as Bible study and a little bit of hope."

Did he know Jesus? "I knew him before, but I got more intimate with him there, because I got to see that I just wasn't the only one needing help. There were more people like me. I didn't feel quite as alone. Because there were other people, as I looked around, in the same situation I'm in."

Raymond said that the Bible study and the mentoring by some of our staff gave him hope and helped him the most during his stay at Joy Junction. It's been my experience that many of our guests feel pretty hopeless when they arrive, and I think it is a combination of being without a home and coping with emotionally and physically debilitating situations that land them in that sad predicament. I was so glad to hear our staff had encouraged him.

He didn't want to say what issues specifically had landed him at Joy Junction, and I never want to press people to share anything they are not comfortable sharing. But Raymond was willing to say that "hard times" in his life resulted in his homelessness. "I come from a family of nine," he said, "and we didn't have much, you know, all my life. I was in foster homes, group homes, and boys' homes, and I just had a hard time."

Good news was on the horizon. Since leaving Joy Junction, Raymond now works at a local hotel, has a studio apartment, and attends a church where he also volunteers. "I'm just giving back, because the Lord has blessed me so much."

I asked Raymond what advice he would have for someone who may be in the depths of despair and is perhaps wondering if he or she could come to Joy Junction or enroll in a recovery program. Without hesitating, he said no one should stay in despair with the existence of Joy Junction and many other programs. "And don't give up, because there's a living God out there. He loves you even if your family doesn't, if your brother doesn't, if your teacher doesn't. Jesus loves you so much."

Raymond added, "I was hopeless all my life, because nobody ever loved me. I come from the projects in Los Angeles, South Central. There was no love in those projects, just drugs, alcohol, and all that stuff. But you know what? I know now that God loves me. He sent his son, Jesus Christ, to die for me. You can't get that kind of love anywhere on this earth. There's nothing else like it. You might search and search all around the world, trying to find the love in people and materialistic things, but there's no love like the love of Jesus Christ."

He encouraged volunteers and donors to keep helping out, adding that doing so "makes you feel wonderful inside, and plus, we're doing the Lord's work. And that's what it's all about. Give because there are so many people out there in need, especially at Joy Junction. They take care of hundreds of women and children, so we need to give to Joy Junction."

That's what we are all about: being used as vessels so God's restorative love can be poured out spiritually and physically upon those in need.

Sheryl

Sheryl enjoyed a good childhood. She was raised in a Christian home and attended Christian schools. But all that was to change when she turned fifteen. Sheryl said, "My innocence was taken away by a rape that ended up being an unwanted pregnancy. Being an adopted child, I put my daughter up for adoption to Christian parents. The pain was too great for me to handle."

Reaction of Christians to the incident hurt Sheryl. She also began questioning how the Lord could allow one of his children to be harmed in such a manner. As a result, she started running from her family and other loved ones, and for years, she kept running. And, as she ran from the Lord, she wound up in the arms of the Enemy.

She said, "I ran to drugs, and this led to men who were abusive mentally, physically, and sexually. It seemed like I could not get away from this type of lifestyle." Sheryl said she finally decided to settle down, get married, and raise a family, thinking her life would change. But it didn't. There was always some kind of abuse from her husband. "I left my husband and three children, returning to my old lifestyle in the dark world of alcohol, drugs, and bikers." The second man Sheryl married was a biker, and once again, she had entered into an abusive relationship. She became his "property." The second marriage soon ended in a violent divorce, and Sheryl was homeless for a time. Her next relationship turned out to be one of more unkept promises. It ended when she was again addicted to drugs and, as she put it, tired of being "broken."

She wanted to find out who she was really destined to be. She knew the answer in her heart but felt she had strayed from that place. In an attempt to fix the damage, Sheryl found herself at the women's division of a gospel mission. She was addicted to pain pills, crack, and marijuana. A staff member suggested she sign up for the mission's rehab program, Family Hope Discipleship, and Sheryl did not hesitate. "I wanted change. I needed to let go and let God do his work in me. About one month later, at a huge church, I accepted Christ back into my life." Two weeks after that, she was baptized in one of the nearby lakes with about eighty other people. "Wow! What an amazing, warm feeling came over me when I came up from the water. I knew the Spirit was in me."

Sheryl did well until she fell in love with a man from the men's discipleship program. After eight months, the two of them were asked to leave. She and her boyfriend did very well for a while, but that was about to change. She said, "Soon, he began to drink, and things started to go down real fast from there." Not long after, Sheryl's boyfriend was diagnosed with third-stage small cell lung cancer. She said, "My faith soared during this time, despite his illness. I quit my job to take care of him full-time. He had become paralyzed, and his speech was slurred. God answered our prayers during this time. Our best friend finally told him, 'You should marry Sheryl. She has gone through so much for you.'"

The two of them got married, and their church raised enough money for his ex-wife and daughter to fly in from Grants, New Mexico, for the wedding. After ten years, he would see his only daughter. "A miracle," Sheryl said. "Just 168 hours later, my husband died in his sleep. I never lost faith during this whole time, even though I was mad at God for taking him from me." Sheryl said in the last three weeks of her husband's life, God brought them back to the gospel mission to be around the friends and teachers they had in rehab. She stayed there for eight months.

Sheryl and her teenage daughter then went to live with her oldest daughter. She stayed single and didn't date for sixteen months. She texted an old friend named John the words "Happy New Year," and a friendship between her and John started to bloom.

She lost her job and could not save her house. Due to stress, she found herself in the hospital, while the courts put a twenty-four-hour quit notice on the house. She lost everything. Sheryl was homeless again. That resulted in Sheryl and John staying with friends for a few weeks.

Meanwhile, John decided to turn himself in for an old DUI in a nearby county. Sheryl returned to the mission once again, leaving every morning to go to work, while her teenage daughter was going to a friend's house and running the streets. After John was released, their troubles increased. They stayed in a rundown hotel in Kalamazoo for about a month. As a result of some bad associations, they received death threats. Sheryl said, "The threats kept coming, and I started having nightmares of John being shot in front of me and dying in my arms." Despite the threats, Sheryl said their faith kept them strong, and they grew closer. John's uncle lived in Tijeras, New Mexico, and he told them to come out. They loaded up their car with all their belongings and headed west.

Things went well for a while. While in Tijeras, John spent his mornings chopping wood and talking to God while Sheryl read Psalms and Proverbs, and then they would both write to God. "I really felt closer to God being in the mountains."

But they left John's uncle's place and came to Joy Junction. "Since being here, we have told people our story and shared with them what

God has done with us. We have tried every day to serve God in all we have done here. Though we have our ups and downs, we do not lose our focus on God."

Where would Sheryl and John have gone without Joy Junction? Sheryl said, "We would have had nowhere to go without Joy Junction; home was not an option. To me, this is a safe haven for myself and for people who are broken in any area of their lives. Here they can find healing. No matter why I'm here, God has been with me. He has never left me, and he never will." Sheryl added, "I feel more comfortable, and my walk is getting stronger every day. My heart is turning into a servant's heart with no questions of why."

Sheryl and John have always stepped up to help other members of the Joy Junction community in need. They do this with a nonjudgmental, humble attitude. What a blessing it is for us to be involved with them and in the lives of all the guests the Lord brings to our doors.

Margie

Margie says that the worst part of being homeless is "when you have to go without food—and when it's just so cold that you can't even bear it, and you don't have enough to wrap up in, and you're losing feeling in your body parts because you're so cold." She is a missionary pastor's daughter and didn't plan to be virtually homeless, living with her husband on the West Mesa in Albuquerque, New Mexico. But that is how she started 2010.

I met Margie some time ago while on an outreach with the Joy Junction Lifeline of Hope mobile feeding unit. She told me how appreciative she was of the supplies we had given her and her husband. She called the unexpected gifts "wonderful."

Margie's life was very difficult due to ongoing pain, a number of surgeries, and a delayed disability assessment. While living in Chicago and working in the medical field, she dislocated her shoulders, tore up her hand, hit her nose, and had to have reconstructive sinus and hand surgeries. Now in Albuquerque as a result of her husband's employment, Margie is undergoing a series of operations.

After Margie's husband left his job, he began traveling and looking for employment. Ultimately, he found work in Albuquerque, but it hasn't been at all easy. There are a lot of barriers to moving into an apartment or a house that people don't necessarily think about, Margie said. "I don't even know my way around Albuquerque. I don't know the good places or the bad ones. How am I going to feel like I'm safe to go off and get an apartment when I don't even know the area?"

Fortunately, she has been able to communicate. "My family bought me a cell phone, and they pay for it so that I can at least get all my doctors' calls. Between that, you know, and them helping me, that's all I get. My unemployment's all gone, and they wouldn't even let me have an extension. They told me I didn't make enough to get an extension."

Margie said the people of Albuquerque have treated her wonderfully. "So much more wonderful than Chicago, where I'm from. I think that's one thing that keeps me out here." To the people who have helped her, such as her husband's employer, she says, "Thank you to everybody who pulled together during the times when I needed it. I didn't have a vehicle when I went in for surgery, so my husband's boss he let him take me to surgery in the service truck. He picked me up in the service truck and gets my medicine in the service truck. There are good people out here."

Margie is also grateful for the Joy Junction donors, whose kindness and generosity allows us to keep the Lifeline of Hope on the road. She said if it weren't for the Lifeline, she would have to wait another month before being able to buy desperately needed supplies. Not having the needed food and supplies is the most difficult thing about being homeless. And at that point, Margie said, "I feel like I'm alone . . . and that nobody cares."

But I reminded her, "We care for you, Jesus cares for you, and a lot of generous donors around town care for you as well."

I asked Margie what hopes she had for the upcoming year. She said she wants to make it through the remainder of her six surgeries and get her disability. "I don't want to be pushed away by the courts any longer because of my age. I'm hurt, and I can't work ever again, even if the surgeries do work."

Margie said her relationship with Jesus enabled her to get through the last year. She said, "Without him, I wouldn't be here. I would have already committed suicide. I can guarantee you that. I have been through such a hard last fifteen months that if it wasn't for the Lord, I would have just said, 'Forget it.'" She encourages everyone who reads her story to believe in God. "If you do, he'll bring you the good people, and that means really believing in God when you're down and out, crying to him. Don't cry to your mom. You really, really have to 100 percent belief, and people will come to you. They will be there to help."

Margie is one of the flock God allows us to reach. It is such a great opportunity to share the love of Jesus Christ tangibly with those who are outside the walls of Joy Junction. Our friends and donors make it possible.

Frank

Traveling the streets of Albuquerque as I used to do at the inception of Joy Junction's Lifeline of Hope route, provided an opportunity to share the spiritual and physical love of Jesus with people the Lord chooses to put in our way. It was such a blessing to share food and essential supplies directly to worried and discouraged people.

Some of these people were involuntarily displaced from an apartment complex that had been closed by the city as substandard. We passed a man sitting on the corner of Menaul and Carlisle with a sign. He had eyes of heartfelt desperation. It was as if they bore into our souls and compelled us to stop. We pulled into a parking lot, introduced ourselves, and asked the man if he was hungry. He said he was, so we gave him a sack lunch and a bottle of vitamin water. He asked for another lunch and water for his friend, which we happily gave. We gave another sack lunch to a man who asked for an extra meal for his friend "who can't get up and come over here." Again, we were happy to oblige. We have found it a common occurrence that many of the homeless are very concerned for their friends and that there is an intense camaraderie between those in need.

Then there's Frank who we met at another location where we feed people. He told me that the Lifeline helps a lot. "Because when I don't got nothing, they always come help me right here. Always," he said.

Frank told me a bit of his story, and he had some pretty good advice about the perils of drinking. He said, "I used to drink hard liquor every day—vodka, whiskey, anything I could get. It almost caused me to lose my family and everything. My wife told me to choose the alcohol or choose my family. I chose my family. I still drink a bit every now and then, but it's nothing like being an alcoholic. At least I'm doing better. I'm getting better at it, and I'm still with my wife for thirty years."

Faith is how Frank has gotten through all the trials in his life. "Faith. Faith in my Lord Jesus Christ, and my wife being on my side. She keeps my best part of me. She makes a difference in me doing better." Frank had experienced some tough love from his wife, of whom he spoke so admiringly. She told him, "You either want me and the kids, or you want to live by yourself and be homeless." Frank said, "I didn't want to be homeless; I love my wife and my kids." As a result, he decided to put his wife and family ahead of alcohol. "I put them first from now on in my life because God blessed me . . . and gave me the strength to do so."

What would Frank say to those thinking of experimenting with alcohol or drugs? "That's not a good thing. You need to recognize it is okay to drink a little bit occasionally, but not to be a drunk. Never be a drunk."

I asked Frank what he sees ahead. He said, "God blessing everybody through my Lord Jesus Christ. Keep your faith in the Lord Jesus Christ, and you'll be all right."

Frank, I couldn't say it better. Thanks for brightening our day when we see you in your part of Albuquerque. I pray you keep serving the Lord and grow in his grace and love.

Food for Thought

Now that you have read stories of some of the real people we have come into contact at Joy Junction, have your prior conceptions of homeless people changed?

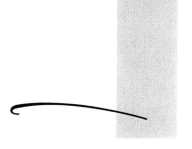

To Worry or Not to Worry? That Is the Question

It's really not helpful, but we all worry.

We worry about sickness, losing our jobs, and lack of finances, and we worry about being worried. But think for a minute how many of the things about which you've worried have come to pass. Maybe a few, but definitely not as many as those about which you worried, right?

I'm an inveterate worrier, and thinking back, I realize a few of the things about which I worried did come to pass, but my worrying didn't influence them or help in any way. It just destroyed my ability to enjoy the present. But I still worry—even though the Bible tells me to cast my cares on God. I'm working on it!

Recently I was thinking about the worries a homeless person might have. If anyone "deserves" to have worries, they do. Denis Billy, our resident services manager, asked a few of our guests what they worried about most.

One woman said that prior to coming to Joy Junction, her biggest worries were not being able to get enough food to eat and finding a safe place to sleep. She said, "I was controlled by fear . . . It's hard trying to get around day by day not knowing what's out there on the streets . . . Another fear is hanging out with the wrong people at the wrong time."

Another woman said she worries about her two young children. "What I'm going through as a homeless person will have an effect on their life, school, health, and immediate needs."

However, she added, this time in their lives has been one of real learning. "We all appreciate everything we used to take for granted. We have had time to really spend time together. We are thankful to everyone that has [occurred]. And we're thankful that we are getting rid of all the bad things in our lives."

Finding a place to lay her head, get her next meal, take a shower, and wash her clothes were all worries of another woman. She confided she also worried about being robbed while she slept.

She continued, "I thank God for Joy Junction. I now have a place to sleep, eat, shower, and a place to wash my clothes. I'm finally off the streets. If it wasn't for Joy Junction, I would still be on the streets."

One of our male guests told us his biggest fear was not having enough money to "survive." He added, "I also worry about not being able to make it in the world every day. This affects me emotionally and mentally. The life of a homeless person is really hard when you're trying to survive the real world . . . It's very scary and hard living on the streets."

Another male guest said the winter months were his biggest worry. "Where am I going to sleep and how would I stay warm? I also worried about where I would eat and get fresh clothes. I learned how to camp out in rest rooms. Then I got smart, and began to sleep in ICU waiting rooms. They offered fold out chairs that turned into beds. I was also given free coffee, TV, and newspapers there."

A female guest had worries that may resonate with many of us. She said her biggest worry as a homeless person is getting back into society and starting her life over. "I want to acquire a home again and secure a job. I don't want to die or get ran over by angry people who don't like homeless people who carry bags around. I also don't want to be labeled as lazy and worthless."

Food for Thought

Whether it's "reality based" or not, worry is very real to the worrier. Believe me, I know. But next time you're worried, please take a minute and think about the worries of a homeless person. So doing might just help you get through yours a little more easily.

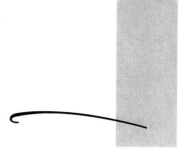

WHEN POVERTY KNOCKS . . .

"When poverty knocks on the door, love flies out the window." That quotation is one I recently heard and it grabbed me the minute I heard it. Do you think that it's true?

Worries about finding shelter and food are intensely real for the homeless. But what about its effect on relationships? I asked Denis Billy, our resident services manager, to find out if it is true.

One woman said after her best friend was murdered, she came to Albuquerque to see her big sister. When her money ran out, worse was to come. "My sister abandoned me and didn't want anything to do with me, because I had nothing to offer her. I was very sad." As a result, she came to Joy Junction.

One male guest said his poverty and consequent homelessness resulted in him finding out "people's bad ways." He continued, "Their attitude changed towards me. Some people would come up and laugh at me. They don't understand the reason for my homelessness. The Lord will get me through this, and I will never take my eyes off of Him."

Another Joy Junction guest said she became homeless at the age of thirty-five, and it changed her life. "I lost a beautiful four-bedroom home.

I lost all sense of safety and security, life, and my world as I knew it. My world was completely turned upside down." She said friends began to judge her and turned their backs on her and her children.

It also affected her family relationships. She said, "They automatically began to judge me and assumed the worst. They never offered to help us. I'm just happy that I still have my kids, and God will never forsake us."

However, it wasn't all bad. Relationships with her children who were four, ten, and fourteen at the time, deepened. She said, "My two older children understood what had happened and knew that we needed to get closer."

One guest said when she first became homeless, her family made the situation even worse. She said they told her, "You lost everything—your home, your family, and your life."

However, that wasn't the case with her relationship with her husband. Homelessness, she said, made her bond with him grow stronger. "Before, we used to fight and blame each other for things. We are now stronger as a couple, because we needed to rely on each other when others abandoned us. We've learned to be more supportive of each other."

A forty-year-old woman said when she became homeless, it affected her relationship with her husband, her kids, and other people around her. It was deeply stressful. "It was an everyday battle trying to figure out how to pay for our hotel room again. Most of the time we would sell drugs to come up with the money, but some days there were not enough sales. I started . . . shoplifting merchandise from stores." She added, "My husband did not approve of me doing this. The stress of getting caught was always his concern. We would argue and blame each other for our situation." Understandably, her behavior and the resulting arguments also affected the kids.

Another guest said while his homelessness hasn't resulted in love flying out the window, it had a big impact on his family. Not just his children and their mother, but also his own mother and sisters. "They worry all of the time about how I'm doing, where I'm at, and if I'm eating well. They especially worry about if I take care of my (self). And . . . if I have a safe place to sleep at night throughout this cold season."

This man said he appreciates all the help he has received from Healthcare for the Homeless and area shelters. "It has helped me to survive a life on the streets," he said.

You can see the answers are a mixed bag for the people we talked to, but there's no doubt that lack of money results in the stress level increasing.

Food for Thought

So what about you? Has poverty knocked on your door? Did love fly out the window? If so, you might have more than a little understanding of the plight faced daily by some of our guests. If not, please say a prayer anyway for those not so blessed.

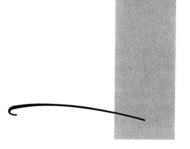

THE CHICKEN, THE EGG, AND "COMORBIDITY"

After reading the varied stories in the previous chapters, I wonder if you are asking yourself some questions about the causes of homelessness.

One question I often hear is: Does mental illness factor into becoming homeless? Related are these questions: Which comes first? Does mental illness lead to homelessness, or do the stresses and struggles that accompany homelessness possibly trigger mental illness?

Then right alongside that question: Does alcoholism result in homelessness, or does the misery of everyday living experienced by many homeless people lead to alcoholism?

On our Facebook page, someone commented that until recently, he would have said it is mental illness that results in people becoming less functional and unable to maintain themselves. He continued, "Statistically speaking, how many psychologically 'normal' people hit the street due to job loss, loss of income, etc., then developed anxiety disorder . . . depression, and even psychotic breaks due to the hopelessness of that amount of poverty?"

It's a good point and one that drew a lot of commentary on Facebook. Angela said it's a "chicken-or-egg" scenario. You know, which came first?

She said becoming homeless would cause many so-called "sane" people to become depressed. She added, "Not being able to provide for yourself or children would cause depression . . . and I am . . . not sure that one is greater than the other or that there is a right answer." However, she said there definitely needs to be more attention for this "epidemic."

Mary said she doesn't think there's a "right" answer. "Mental illness will inevitably cause a person to become homeless without any love or support. A healthy person will inevitably have their breaking point and have a mental breakdown being homeless without love and support. So the more support we can give, the more we can educate ourselves, the more we can find a solution to homelessness."

Celia said for her, addiction brought on mental health issues. "I became depressed, anxious, hopeless, isolated, and then homeless because I had used up my family and friends and their patience. Next step was homelessness, which in itself caused more of the mental [health issues]. I've found other avenues to reduce stress and anxiety without resorting to slip and go back to my addiction. That's always there, so once again, I'm back to the stress and anxiety and still homeless."

Stephenie said there's no clear answer as to which comes first, as the situation can go both ways. She said that mental illness can come first and cause someone's life to spiral out of control, "especially if they don't seek help or don't recognize the warning signs of mental illnesses." As a result, people end up losing their jobs, homes, car, and push themselves away from friends and family. "Then they eventually become homeless and on the streets. Many people with mental illness will also self-medicate with drugs and alcohol, and that can lead to homelessness."

Conversely, Stephenie continued, "The stress of losing your job, livelihood, and car can trigger depression and anxiety and result in homelessness."

Joanna said when you feel hopeless and the feeling of normal "isn't there" for you any more, depression and anxiety start to set in. When that happens, you start falling apart. The pain inside of you is horrific." She added, "We lose ourselves, and everyone that was in our lives will lose us also. Digging yourself out of that dark hole takes everything you have inside of you."

Rachel said the question being addressed is known technically as *comorbidity*. She added, "One can contribute to the other and it can go both ways. For statistics, there is a book called *Social Injustice and Public Health* (second edition), by Barry Levy, which addresses both homelessness and mental health. Two separate chapters, but the homelessness chapter addresses mental health and the mental health chapter addresses homelessness."

And what about substance abuse and homelessness? Which one causes the other? The same person who asked the question about mental illness commented, "I think if one was freezing cold, hungry, feeling suicidal/hopeless, that *anything* available to relieve some of that pain would be welcomed."

She proposed the scenario of someone sitting against a building, their feet hurting badly from walking around all day, and their back and joints hurting from arthritis or fibromyalgia. She continued, "You felt that things could and would never get better, and you were sitting there grieving the loss of your children or pets due to your homeless situation and someone offered you a substance that you knew would make you care a bit less about it, wouldn't it be tempting to alleviate the pain a little?"

Danielle said her ex-husband has been through all of this, losing everything because of addiction that all started with a back injury. She said, "He is clean now and taking his mental health meds but still on the streets of New Mexico sleeping in the cold."

So while I don't have an answer to the question I posed at the beginning of this chapter, here's a good piece of advice. Whether someone is homeless because of mental illness, alcoholism, or purely economic reasons, our place is to encourage and help—not judge.

Knowing the Facts

An Albuquerque man who told a panhandler to "Go get a f–ing job," recently got more than he expected.

The victim, who said he didn't want to use his name for safety concerns, told KOB-TV's Kai Porter, "I turn this way, and he's coming at me, and he struck me, broke my glasses . . . and then we started tumbling, and I put him in a head lock."

KOB said the man added, "I managed to get my phone out with my other hand and called 911. So I had an active 911 call going on, and then about that time he tried to grab a knife, I dropped the phone, held his hand down, and was screaming for help."

Police finally showed up and arrested the panhandler, KOB reported. The victim took a picture of a syringe he said fell out of the man's pocket.

Is it safe to say that the panhandler quite likely had some mental health issues? Do we need to look beyond the panhandling to the laws regulating certain behaviors occurring as a result of mental illness?

It is unlikely that such a person would follow the advice on all the numerous blue signs that have sprouted up around to call the city's 311 hotline. And if he or she did, what could the operators do? This seems to be a case way beyond the ability of 311 or shelters.

Facebook friends of Joy Junction quickly weighed in after I asked them what they thought.

Kelly said, "Had the man responded to the panhandler in a more respectful fashion, chances are he would have had no reason to become physically violent."

Jerry commented, "Maybe this man has tried to get a job or is not employable. And Albuquerque's little blue signs are not much help, especially for the mentally ill. Positive solutions need to be found."

Terry said when people are cold and hungry, the best thing to do is to be kind. "I have a job and a home, but am getting older and when it is very cold out and I have to be out in it, my bones hurt . . . Think about people who are trying to figure things out and having to be there all day until they can get it together. The victim could have just said, 'I'm sorry but no.' The 'F' word brings about ugliness, no matter who it is directed to."

Mary seemed to understand, saying that many panhandlers have issues that prevent them from getting a job. She added, "This guy [the victim] is a jerk. If you don't want to give them any money, a simple 'No' or 'Not today' is sufficient."

Liz echoed that sentiment, saying a simple, "'I'm sorry, I don't have any money' would've done." She added, "Instead he thought it was appropriate to demean and be disrespectful to the panhandler. Respect is a two way street . . . Looks like he got what he deserved, and the panhandler got a free night's stay in a warm place and a meal."

Commenting on the KOB website, Thebes said, "The junkie panhandler he insulted was probably too mentally ill to 'get a f#^%ing job.'" He added, "I'm not saying the junkie should have beaten him up, just that if we dealt with mental illnesses as a disease rather than the mentally ill as criminals—this probably never would have happened."

John reminded readers the law is unable to deal with mental health issues. It is basically against the law to hold anyone without their consent, and getting an order of involuntary commitment is not an easy matter. "This 'violation of their civil rights' has been going on since the 1970s, which is why most mental hospitals in this country were shut down."

Some thoughts: Our insistence on giving the homeless mentally ill their so-called civil rights will end up pushing some of them right into an early grave and ruining the lives of innocent citizens along the way. We have a responsibility to educate ourselves about issues besetting our community. The homeless in general, and the homeless mentally ill in particular, are those about whom we should be concerned, not shout profanities at.

I am not condoning the attack, but as Gary said on Facebook, the "victim" shouldn't have provoked the panhandler. He added, "People ought to know that a loose mouth might get popped. Solomon said as much, too, didn't he? 'A fool's lips enter into contention, and his mouth calleth for strokes'" (Prov. 18:6 KJV).

It's time we talked about a real solution before someone gets really hurt—again.

Alcoholism and the Homeless: a Sin or a Disease?

We live in an alcohol-saturated culture where the link is often made between drinking alcohol and having a good time.

Unless you're a fundamentalist, conservative American Christian, or over-consume alcohol, drinking, unlike smoking, is a socially-acceptable behavior. There's usually a drink available at many after-hours business networking functions as well as numerous other events.

People drink for a variety of reasons—some because they like the taste, others to unwind, and perhaps a number because they don't want to be perceived as different from others in their group.

A Google search for the word *alcohol* produced about 415,000,000 results. Putting the words *alcoholic beverages* into Google turned up about 18,600,000 options.

Some people may argue the overwhelmingly popular genre of country music, with its long history of drinking songs, encourages drinking. Country singer Brad Paisley released a song in May 2005 called "Alcohol." *Wikipedia* describes the song, "Paisley personifies alcoholic beverages in general, describing the various influences that the beverages have on certain people ('Helping white people dance'), ultimately stating 'You'll have some of the best times you'll never remember, with me, Alcohol.'"

But what about those who don't drink to have a good time, but do so to escape the miserable circumstances and other pain they're experiencing in their lives? The first few drinks are "options," then the addiction sets in. Are these individuals "sinning," or is there something more going on? Sometimes we come up with a bumper-sticker solution for a problem that's much more complex.

I wanted a quick, non-random, unscientific survey, so I turned to our Joy Junction Facebook page and asked this question.

"So is alcoholism a sin, an addiction/disease, or both, and how should we best deal with it? In addition, are some people genetically predisposed to alcoholism?" I also wrote, "At Joy Junction we have a Christ-centered, nine-month life recovery program, which is based on the Tyndale House Life Recovery Bible. The program is an integral part of what we do at Joy Junction. It is long on love and answers and short on condemnation."

As I expected, the answers were varied and all over the map. Some were disturbing, simplistic, and troubling.

Kathy commented that alcoholism is not a disease but an addiction. "It is a wicked sin, just like drug addiction. You can get victory over it with the help of Jesus. The first thing to do is turn your life over to Jesus to save your soul. The Holy Spirit will help you . . . "

Evelyn said, "Alcoholism comes from gluttony! Stemmed from the relief in letting go of unpleasant things, realities one chooses to forget.

Juli said alcoholism is a choice. "I know because I'm an alcoholic, and I chose to do so knowing how addictive it is. People always try to make excuses—own up and deal with it."

Mary said, "The flesh wants what it wants. When we feed it, it grows. Do not feed it [and] the desire dies—simple. Using genetics or predisposition just makes it easier to explain. It is the desire of the flesh which can be overcome with the help of the Spirit."

Carol was more balanced. She said with God's help and a desire by the person suffering to want to stop drinking, the battle against alcoholism can be won. She said alcoholism is, "No different than smoking or any other addiction, unless, of course, the drug has altered the mind to the point of complete destruction where there is no ability to think."

John Paul said he believes addiction is a disease. He continued, "Crying out for help is a life-changing moment. For me, this produced a direct experience of the Holy Spirit. God saved me, and I believe He will save anyone who reaches out for Him" He added, "That said, I know some atheists who have recovered by practicing 12-step spiritual principles (honesty, hope, love, service, and so forth). I believe God makes recovery available to everyone, regardless of religious belief."

Andy Bales, the CEO of Union Rescue Mission in Los Angeles, had an interesting response. He said his type 1 diabetes is an inherited disease. However, he continued, "I am responsible to manage it, and if I don't and rebel and let it run wild, that would be a sin."

So what's my take? It's very simple. Don't think you know the answer and that people could quit drinking if they really wanted to. Learn their story by getting to know them, and before you condemn them for taking a drink in the first place, ask yourself if you could have endured what they have quite probably experienced in their lives. You might have ended up drinking more than they have.

The power of the Holy Spirit is still more than sufficient to deliver, and why that happens in some cases and not others is still a mystery to me. We will probably never know this side of eternity. Until then, let's do the loving and leave any judging up to God. He does a much better job at it than we do.

Food for Thought

I hope it is evident by this time there are many reasons for a person ending up homeless. Mental illness and addiction are just two of them. Can you think of a way to help solve at least one reason for homelessness?

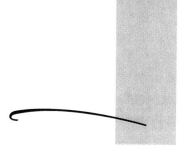

HUNGER IS NOT JUST CONFINED TO ONE CULTURAL GROUP

There's enough of a hunger problem in New Mexico that the noise you hear sometimes may not be your neighbor trying to start his car. It could be his growling stomach.

According to the New Mexico Association of Food Banks, nearly 70,000 New Mexicans seek food assistance weekly. That's the equivalent of a city the size of Santa Fe needing emergency assistance every week.

Between 30 and 40 percent of the members of households seeking food assistance are children under the age of eighteen, and 21 percent of the people seeking food assistance in New Mexico are senior citizens.

Sixty-one percent of households report that in the previous year they had to choose between paying utilities or buying food. Of this group, 33 percent reported they have to make this tough choice every month. Forty-eight percent of households report having to choose between paying their rent or mortgage or buying food, and 19 percent of this group are forced to make this choice every month.

Sometimes we forget that behind the statistics are hungry people with growling stomachs. My own experiences also helped me empathize with the many homeless and hungry clients who continue to be served by Joy Junction. Did you know between our Lifeline of Hope mobile feeding units and meals we serve at our South Valley facility that we provide more than 16,000 meals each month? Clients often say that it's the only meal they've eaten (or expect to eat) for the day. They're so appreciative.

People often ask me whether hunger and homelessness are increasing. It's hard to give a definitive answer about homelessness, but based upon the number of people we feed, I would say hunger is definitely a growing problem.

I wanted to help further personalize hunger for you, so I asked our resident services manager at Joy Junction to find out from a few of our guests what it felt like. They were quick to respond.

One man said when he's been hungry for a while he feels "weak and sad, a little depressed." He recalled one time not eating for twelve hours. When he finally got food, "I ate too much and vomited. I don't remember where the meal came from. I was just so happy." He sees evidence of New Mexico's hunger problem statewide. "I don't like seeing people hungry. Thank God for Joy Junction. I wish more people would donate more money and food here. We need it." He said Joy Junction feeds him well. There was an interesting caveat. "I may not like all of the meals, but at least I'm not going hungry like so many others."

Another man said he's always hungry when he doesn't make it to Joy Junction, but he appreciates the food when he gets there. He recalled a recent meal at the shelter. "It was great. I don't even remember what it was. It could've been dog . . . [crap] for all I care. I was starving."

And hunger in New Mexico? "Kind of a dumb question. Of course there's a hunger problem. But, I don't know how to fix it. Just keep feeding people here. You're doing a good job, I guess. You have fed me, housed me, clothed me. Keep doing what you're doing."

A man who at time of writing has stayed at Joy Junction for a month said, "Everyone has been hungry." He continued, "We feel tired and weak. We feel depressed. We feel like losers. Joy Junction has helped me with getting food. I'm glad now. I don't feel so bad now that I have a place to call home. If we built more places like Joy Junction, we wouldn't have a hunger problem."

One Joy Junction guest said, "Since I've been here now for a week or so I've fattened up. After eating here, I felt normal again." She added, "New Mexico doesn't take care of the homeless. Joy Junction helps the homeless. I can't even get food stamps . . . Thanks for feeding me. I got a clothing voucher yesterday. I don't know how to thank you. Jesus is at Joy Junction."

Another guest said she has been hungry. When this woman's stomach cries out for food, it makes her physically tired and weak, as well as emotionally sad and angry. She continued, "When I eat here after I've been gone for a while, I feel happy and thankful."

This woman said that it's not just New Mexico, but America has a hunger problem. "People don't want to help the poor," she said. "Panhandlers are made fun of. I was panhandling last week and someone gave me their trash instead of cash. They laughed and drove off. People don't give a s—t! I'm glad that I have a place to eat here."

One woman said she appreciates the food at Joy Junction, describing it as "great." She added, "I'm not sure how the hunger issue is here in New Mexico. I'm pretty sure it's bad since we need a place like Joy Junction. I have no idea how to fix it. Maybe we need more food banks and shelters."

One man, who described himself as "growing up on the reservation," had a different perspective. He said, "We don't go hungry there because everyone feeds you. There are no homeless on the reservation. Did you know that?"

However, it's different when you come to the city and lose your job, he said. That's when you go hungry. "That's what happened to me. But, now I'm an outcast back home. They all are ashamed of me. I felt pretty grateful for getting food after going without for so long. Someone gave me a turkey leg last year from the state fair." Almost reflectively he added, "Joy Junction is a lifeline of hope. It's just like the truck says."

I was curious to learn more about hunger on the Indian reservations. The Indian Relocation Act of 1956 (also known as Public Law 959 or the Adult Vocational Training Program) was a United States law intended to encourage Native Americans in the United States to leave Indian reservations, acquire vocational skills, and assimilate into the general population.

This program played a significant role in increasing the population of urban American Indians in succeeding decades.

However, as Denis Billy, our Native American resident services manager said, "This program was very helpful for some but became a detriment for others. Many American Indians fell victim to alcoholism and drug addiction. Those who failed at a life in the city returned to the reservation in shame. Their addictions continued on the reservation, and, for some, took their life of addiction back from whence it came."

Billy said, as such he agreed with the statement above from our Native American guest. He added, "Back in the 60's, my mother worked with a program in San Francisco and Oakland. She assisted American Indians with learning to live in the city—a huge contrast from the reservation."

According to one article, while there may be food on many reservations, there is a lack of nutritional items, resulting in older Native Americans being hit particularly hard.

The same article said the U.S. Department of Agriculture considers most reservations "food deserts"—low-income areas where many people lack access to nutritional foods.

According to the Center for Rural Health, about six in ten Native Americans age fifty-five and older, survive on between $5,000 and $10,000 a year. The combination of rampant poverty and low-quality food hits tribal elders particularly hard.

Another man told us during his time of homelessness in Texas, he felt he was all alone, emotionally and physically, with no one to help. Eating his first meal after being hungry, he said, was "a very happy feeling."

He said he feels there is a definite hunger issue in New Mexico, and the state should build more homeless shelters."

This man and many others were appreciative of everything they have received at Joy Junction.

Food for Thought

If you live in New Mexico, what can be done to help quell hunger here? I agree with the New Mexico Association of Food Banks. We need to educate ourselves and others about hunger.

I suspect New Mexico is not alone in its general ignorance about how to alleviate hunger and homelessness. What do you know about your state's programs?

While we will almost certainly never end the universality of hunger as we know it, we can "end" hunger one meal at a time. Elma and I, two hearts with one vision, encourage you to see and act upon the vision God gives you about how you can help, one person at a time.

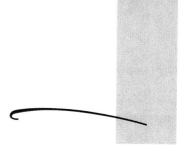

NOT YOUR TYPICAL GRADUATIONS

"**I**f I hadn't done the program and gotten sober, I would have spent the rest of my life homeless and high, or drunk. Now I have a future." What a wonderful comment from one of Joy Junction's recent graduates of the Christ in Power Program.

It wasn't your typical graduation, and the certificate issued won't transfer for any academic credit. But the ceremony was a wonderful experience and the certificate marks the successful completion of nine months of walking the long road to recovery.

The graduation was a celebration of the dedication and accomplishment of six participants of Joy Junction's nine-month, faith-based life-recovery course called Christ in Power Program (CIPP). The curriculum involves classes, Bible study, and volunteer assignments.

Joy Junction is typically thought of as being a homeless shelter, a place where needy people can find a place to stay and enjoy a warm, nourishing meal. While that is very important, there is much more to it than that. While we shelter and feed people and provide an array of other services, we also offer the recovery CIPP program.

CIPP participants are taught the skills they need to reenter and succeed in the workplace. They learn, for example, anger management, healthy eating habits, resumé writing, and a variety of important coping mechanisms.

It is rewarding to hear of renewed hopes and dreams of our graduates, to glean from them what their most memorable moment in the program was, and to see their sense of accomplishment. Joel Steen, program instructor, asked some of the graduates what the CIPP meant to them. First up was Roberta, who called the graduation ceremony wonderful, said the program allowed her "to see that Jesus Christ's spirit truly does exist through some human beings who have good intentions to help people who want to get their life back into focus and become reacquainted with Jesus Christ and God's blessings." She added, "CIPP also helps people who have never known that God and Jesus Christ are true and real."

Karen, who had previously attempted the CIPP but dropped out, said working the program meant the difference for her between living and dying. "If I hadn't done the program and gotten sober, I would have spent the rest of my life homeless and high, or drunk. Now I have a future." She also enjoyed the ceremony, saying "It gave a sense of accomplishment, because for the first time I did the program clean and sober."

Ashley is another graduate of the program, which she said helped her get back on track to recovering from her co-dependency. "I understand that I will have to continue working the twelve steps in order to stay 'sober' from my tendency towards unhealthy relationships. The step that stands out the most in my life now is step eleven, 'praying only for the knowledge of God's will and the power to carry it out.'"

Ashley said the nine months all the way through to the graduation ceremony made her feel cared for and loved, and that the kindness of the Joy Junction staff could really be felt.

Lia said her participation in CIPP showed her a new life. "I never used to pray before. I was embarrassed. I used to not have a relationship with God. Now I know I do. I'm still working on forgiveness. I learned I need to forgive even when I don't want to." Lia appreciated the graduation ceremony because, "It felt good to know people recognized you for what you've done. It was an accomplishment."

A former resident services manager said working in the program is never easy for him and the other Joy Junction staff. "It's a sifting and purifying process that hurts yet heals," he said. "As the principal instructor, I, too, go through some of the same learning and pruning as the other participants when I share my story of pain and God's deliverance and goodness. Ultimately, we all find, as our new CIPP shirts proclaim, 'Life is tough, but God is good.'"

Another Special CIPP Graduation

There was another ceremony for thirteen program graduates. Some of them shared how the program had touched their lives. Frank said the graduation ceremony gave him a feeling of respect and more. It taught him to keep on going, even when the going got hard. "When doing something to better myself, I've learned not to give up but to always go forward. Even if it is hard, I need to continue what I started. Now that I have graduated, I know I can achieve and accomplish what I thought was too hard."

Andrea said, "Graduation meant seeing a number of people working together to reach a goal to overcome addictive behaviors." She said God helped her successfully graduate from the program, and so did the other program participants.

For Deana, CIPP graduation was very important, as it was only the third time in her life she had successfully followed through to the conclusion of a goal. "It meant a sense of accomplishment. Going through this nine-month program, completing it, and graduating made me feel like I can accomplish anything I set my mind to. It also gave me a sense of pride, because I saw my friends and family's faces, and I knew they were proud." Deana said it wasn't an easy program. "There were many times I wanted to quit. But I stuck it out and made it through. So going through this graduation helped me realize what a strong person I have become. I stuck it out for nine months, and I am a better person today because of this program and the staff here at Joy Junction."

Our other life recovery program participants who have yet to graduate were also in the audience. The ceremony touched Louis. He said when he graduates it will mean "the completion of a goal and the beginning of a new phase in my life." He added, "Dr. Reynalds has found a way through our Lord to make Joy Junction a shelter every other mission in America should emulate. The CIPP program has not only saved me but changed my life completely. For someone who has been agnostic his entire life to be saying what I say now about my belief in Jesus as my Lord and Savior, proves that if you want your life bad enough, this program works. You just have to want it and have a little faith."

Barbara said when she graduates CIPP, she will have "the knowledge and resources to continue on a path of sober living and a change of lifestyle." She also said, "Completing the twelve-step program will help me earn the respect of my children as they are also hurting as a result of a broken family and separation. This will help my marriage and getting my family back together."

Caroline said that her graduation will mean "my heart and soul have been filled with the love of God. I will be able to accomplish anything that I set out to do. I will feel like I can face and conquer the world with my head up and with a smile on my face."

The graduation ceremony was a wonderful experience, and God's presence and blessing was evident.

Food for Thought

Would you pray for all our graduates as well as those who are still making their way through the Christ in Power Program?

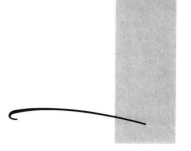

A HAND UP!

We all see the homeless on a daily basis on the streets of Albuquerque. Some are panhandling, attempting to eke out a "living." Others walk and walk and walk, carrying both visible and invisible burdens, trying to pass the time before they are allowed back into to a shelter.

What about those who are stable enough to look for employment? In our current economy, it is hard enough finding work when one has a base of operations like a house and at least a limited amount of income. The normal job-hunting hassles experienced by the unemployed can become almost insurmountable obstacles when one is homeless.

With that in mind, Joy Junction developed an innovative program tailored for those needing less help than that offered by our Christ in Power Life Recovery Program (CIPP). We call it the Hand Up Program (HUP). HUP is a six-month program designed for residents of Joy Junction who are stable enough to look for employment and housing. Participants meet with their case manager at least twice a week to discuss their progress and problems.

One participant said, "Hand Up is good. We are able to connect with people who can help us find employment. Since coming back to

Joy Junction my spouse has already found a job, and I have decided to go back and get my GED."

Another participant said the program is "helping me get a job and go forward with my life. I am going to go through all six months, and hope I get a job soon. It is also helping me find a place of my own, so I can get my son back in my life."

A third person has said, "This program has helped me try and find work. It gives me a place to sleep after a hard day of looking for a job and housing, and I can store my stuff to be able to look for work. I would recommend it to those who need help finding a job."

The goal of the Hand Up Program is to work with the participant's strengths to overcome barriers to finding employment and housing as well as to provide links with other social services in the greater Albuquerque area. In addition to teaching participants how to actively look for employment and housing, HUP participants are required to volunteer for about twelve hours a week at Joy Junction. In addition to having their basic room and board needs met, program participants who comply with the program rules receive a small weekly stipend of ten dollars and the use of a small locker.

Applicants for the program must be at least eighteen years of age, be homeless, have no violent criminal history, and be drug and alcohol free for at least one year. They should also be mentally and physically stable enough to seek employment and have the willingness to take the steps needed to ensure stability at the end of the six-month program.

Carol is an example of how the program works. She came to Joy Junction after not being able to pay her rent due to a cut in her hours at work. Carol was eventually evicted, and she joined the Hand Up Program. HUP helped Carol save enough money to allow her to move into her own apartment. Carol said that Hand Up was a great help, as it allowed her to continue working as a security guard and have a safe place to stay as well as providing her food and the use of our thrift store if she needed clothing.

Carol's success shows what Hand Up can do to help people break the cycle of homelessness. Our prayer is that the Hand Up Program will be a step toward stability and a purposeful life outside the gates of Joy Junction.

Food for Thought

What is the difference between giving someone a handout and giving the person a hand up? How can we take our Christian faith from prayer to action?

ENDURING A
WALK OF SHAME

We've all seen the homeless walking city streets, carrying their bags, pushing a shopping cart, or struggling under the weight of a heavy backpack. Young or old, clean-shaven or bearded, male or female, most of these poor souls have a look of tired desperation.

In downtown Albuquerque we see them so much they almost blend into the landscape. Often they become invisible to us, and when we do "see" them, we really don't see them at all—at least not who they are. Do we ever wonder what is behind the haggard, weary exterior? We try rationalizing our often-judgmental attitude and lack of involvement with thoughts like, *These people are crazy,* or *They are lazy, shiftless people trying to avoid work,* or *They are probably alcoholics or drug addicts.*

How do the bag-carrying homeless feel about transporting all their belongings around with them wherever they go? We asked some of the members of Joy Junction's life-recovery program who used to face that plight on a daily basis.

Their candid answers are surprising. Reflecting back on the experience, one Joy Junction resident said, "It felt like a huge walk of shame, like a ball and a chain in humiliation for the entire world to stare and see. It makes you stick out like a sore thumb. Others look on at you oddly as if you did the worst thing in human history, like you are a monster. They wonder what you'll do next. Each day you think just what it is you can discard to lighten the weight. Maybe I don't need this, or maybe I don't need that. It would be nice to do without all the tiresome weight I carry for long distances."

Someone else said, "I felt like an overburdened vagabond."

Another resident was embarrassed about toting all his belongings around. "You could not leave it anywhere, because it would get stolen. People look at you funny."

One person called the bag-toting experience "degrading." He said, "When I was walking somewhere, I would get the feeling people knew I was homeless. By the time I got to my destination. I would be so tired I would have to rest for thirty minutes just to get my energy back."

Someone else said, "Just imagine having to carry everything you own every day. Not only did I do that, but I also carried my spouse's belongings. It made for a long day."

"When you carry your stuff around people look at you differently, and it's almost impossible to find a job," another individual recalled. "When you walk into a place of employment with all your belongings, you already prove yourself unreliable, because that's how people judge you."

And on that same note, someone else said carrying all your bags around with you made the possibility of getting a job very remote. He added, "No one wants to hire a person who comes in with a bunch of bags."

When these individuals joined Joy Junction's Christ in Power life-recovery program, there was an added benefit they may not have immediately thought about. Not only was there food, shelter, encouragement, and access to bathrooms, there was no more carting, rolling, or pushing their bags around town. Program members have a place at Joy Junction to stash their belongings, and they are all appreciative of this. As one woman said, "I was relieved of the burden of carrying the bags with me, as well as the rush of finding a job. I know I will have to look for a job when my program is over, but I won't have to look like a bag lady doing so." Her friend said, "I get to store my stuff, and I'm not so tired from lugging it around all day. And people don't look at me the same way."

Someone else had an interesting perspective: "Having a locker and a place to live without having to leave every day has taken away some of the stress of being alone." Another person agreed: "By being able to have a home base and being able to clean up, it gives me the confidence to think of myself as employable and valuable to society."

In addition to feeling loved and wanted, isn't that what most of us desire—to be employable and valuable to society? So please don't ignore the next bag-carrying or cart-toting homeless person. Consider getting involved in his or her life by saying a prayer, at the very least, and maybe giving them a fast-food gift card or making a referral to Joy Junction.

Your kindness may be all that's needed to start the person on the road to recovery.

Food for Thought

Would the world look any better if we Christians followed God's command to bless and serve the poor? "If anyone has material possessions and sees a brother or sister in need but has no pity on them, how can the love of God be in that person?" (1 John 3:17).

THANKSGIVING MEMORIES

Joy Junction's Thirtieth Thanksgiving

Thanksgiving Day 2015 marked the thirtieth successive year we shared the blessing of Thanksgiving with Albuquerque's many homeless and abused women and homeless families. I'm thankful to the Lord and our wonderful family of donors for helping make this ministry of compassion possible.

I wondered what difference Joy Junction really makes in the life of some of our guests. We asked a few of them.

One woman said, "I am very thankful for Joy Junction and the Christ in Power (CIPP) life recovery program. If it wasn't for the CIPP program, I would probably still be using and/or be in jail. CIPP is exactly what I need to keep me sober, learn how to have stability, and get closer to God."

Another guest was also very appreciative for Joy Junction. She said, "It's a safe, warm place where I can get fed every day and I'm not in harm's way. I'm thankful for (CIPP) . . . I've been sober for nine months, and I'm planning on going to school after I graduate from Joy Junction. I thank God for that."

Another woman said she's thankful for her three children, all doing well. She's also grateful for Joy Junction. She added, "I am most grateful for a bed to sleep in, three good meals daily, and most of all, being surrounded by caring, loving people. I don't feel alone anymore. And, for what it's worth, I will soon be sixty-nine, and I am realizing the value of friendship and kind words."

She concluded by saying that she is also grateful for Denis Billy, our resident services manager, and former chaplain, Gene Shiplet, who passed on to be with the Lord in late 2015. She said she was learning something new from the chaplain "each and every day."

Another guest was also thankful for Chaplain Gene. He said, "I'm thankful for 'Chappy.' When I first came to JJ and was accepted in CIPP, [Gene] told me that there was a whole staff of people here who would love me unconditionally. It had been so long since I'd felt the love and caring of a parent figure in my life." He added that he's also thankful for the "safety and a soft place to fall here at Joy Junction. I'm not being sappy when I say this. I've never been homeless, and I was terrified of the idea of being on the streets of a major metro."

At Joy Junction, we are a faith-based ministry and believe a relationship with Jesus Christ is the most important component for homeless people in getting back on their feet again. Many of our guests appreciate that philosophy, especially those who join CIPP.

One woman said, "The 12-Step, Bible-based program has made a huge difference in my life. I know that I am a valued person to God, and I can be a better person and be productive only with God's help and my submission to his will and his words."

She added, "I am so thankful for being able to have the time to work on myself here at Joy Junction. I have found there are so many people and resources dedicated just for that purpose. I have been forever changed for the better and am looking forward to more healthier changes in my life."

A man commented, "I'm thankful for God and His precious son, Jesus Christ who died for our sins. I have salvation and forgiveness. I'm set free. I'm also thankful for the people of JJ and my loved ones that he's blessed me with." He said he is grateful for the various situations—good, bad, and hard—he has encountered in his life. He said they have made him the person he is today. And due to some situations, he added, "I was blessed with Joy Junction and the staff who help run it. This place helped me grow."

So . . . what am I thankful for? For our donors, people such as you, for our dedicated staff, for watching people go from despair and addiction to hope and freedom; and for my special recent blessing: Elma, my wife and partner in ministry. To slightly paraphrase 2 Corinthians 9:15, thanks be to God for his indescribable gifts!

Thanksgiving: a Day of Both Sad and Happy Memories

It is hard for me to believe that Thanksgiving Day 2016 will represent over three decades of sharing the blessing of Thanksgiving with Albuquerque's many homeless persons, families, and abused women. I am so thankful to the Lord and our wonderful family of donors for helping make this ministry of compassion possible on an ongoing basis.

Thanks to you, our supporters, we have been able to serve many thousands of hot and nutritious meals to hungry people, minister to many spiritually needy men, women, boys, and girls in our chapel services and life-recovery classes, and provide thousands of nights of shelter to homeless people.

We give thanks to the Lord for all his blessings on Thanksgiving Day and throughout the holiday season, as we provide special meals and activities for our homeless guests.

But not everyone sees things the way we do. For many people, Thanksgiving is not a time to give thanks to God. Take, for example, these Thanksgiving "offerings" I found some years ago from America On Line, billed as "All the Essentials for a Stress-Free Holiday." Encouraged to "sit back and relax," AOL surfers learned they could find "advice on roasting a perfect bird, crafts for the kids, ideas for giving back, hints for handling holiday stress, tips for avoiding the travel crush and much more."

But, if you didn't go any further than the stress section, you would have missed a lot. There were a couple of forums on this AOL Thanksgiving special, one titled "Thanksgiving's Best and Worst," and another giving surfers the opportunity to say what they were most thankful for. Curious to see what people loved and hated about Thanksgiving, I went over first to Thanksgiving's best and worst. I got an inside look at what was on the minds of some Americans that year.

Here are some examples of what I read. One forum participant wrote, "Thanksgiving is easily the most boring day of the year." Someone else commented, "Every year, my house (which is always neat and tidy) gets 'trashed,' even after I've told my in-laws and their kids repeatedly to respect me and our house. My husband sits by and doesn't say a word. I can't turn them away, because they come from out of state and my husband thinks they do no wrong. I'm ready to move to Alaska where I know they'd never visit."

The saddest post of all was from someone who wrote, "This is my first Thanksgiving without my husband of twenty-five years. He left me and our five kids (earlier this year) and served me with dissolution papers soon after." What a testimony that this woman was still grateful for the blessings she had. She continued, "Through this horrible experience, I pray my Thanksgiving is filled with the gratitude and offerings to God that it should be. I am thankful for the gifts I have received, but pray that God's will is to return my husband to me and our children. I would appreciate any prayers, silent or aloud at your Thanksgiving table, for the healing of my family and all other families enduring pain and heartache."

Examples of people writing about what they were most thankful for included an inspiring post from someone who doesn't mind getting older. She wrote, "I used to dread growing older, but now I actually feel as if I can embrace it. When I was younger it was always a case of watching after the kids, stressing over everything always being 'perfect,' trying to prove myself to everyone, but now I have grown to be thankful that I had those times. I also have many things to look forward to."

The letter that really touched my heart was a daughter's tribute to her dad. She wrote: "My father passed away this year. He was a quiet gentleman. I learned much by his words but far more by his actions. He served his country during WWII. He did not speak much about his experiences. Instead he flew our country's flag proudly, reverently. His eyes welled up with tears when he stood for our national anthem. He stood even to the day he needed my mother on one side and myself on the other. He placed flags on the grave sites of each of my brothers, who also served our country. My father is a genuine patriot, and his legacy lives on through all who knew him. I love you Daddy, and I'm thankful and proud to be your daughter."

Some forum participants also remembered the essence of Thanksgiving. Someone wrote, "I am thankful for the Lord for giving me good health, all my children home and in good health, and his mercy." Another person commented, "I am most thankful for allowing Christ to be my guide. I am also thankful for my mental and physical health. I give God all the praise."

After all, that is what Thanksgiving is really all about, isn't it? In case you are not familiar how the day came into existence, here's a quick synopsis. It was way back in 1789 that President George Washington proclaimed a national day of Thanksgiving. This was the first-ever presidential proclamation issued in the United States, and here is how some of it read:

> Whereas it is the duty of all nations to acknowledge the providence of Almighty God, to obey His will, to be grateful for His benefits, and humbly to implore His protection and favor; and whereas both Houses of Congress have by their joint committee, requested me to recommend to the people of the United States a day of public thanksgiving and prayer . . .

Even back then, not everyone was in favor of this National Day of Thanksgiving. It took seventy-four years and President Lincoln to set things straight. In his 1863 proclamation, Lincoln proclaimed the last Thursday of November as a national day of Thanksgiving. After describing America's blessing, Lincoln wrote, "No human counsel has devised nor has any mortal hand worked out these great things. They are the gracious gifts of the Most High God, who while dealing with us in anger for our sins, hath nevertheless remembered mercy."

Lincoln also encouraged his fellow citizens to praise the Almighty for his blessings and to exercise "humble penitence for our national perverseness and disobedience . . . and to fervently implore the (intervention) of the Almighty Hand to heal the wounds of the nation and restore it as soon as may be consistent with the Divine purposes to the full enjoyment of peace, harmony, tranquility and union."

Since that time, Thanksgiving has been proclaimed by every president. So as we get closer to Thanksgiving Day, take a moment and thank the Lord for the many blessings that we enjoy.

Food for Thought

What is your Thanksgiving "offering"? What do you like the best and the least about the Thanksgiving holiday tradition? Why is or why isn't a relationship with Jesus Christ the most important component for homeless people in getting back on their feet.

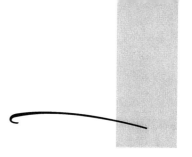

CHRISTMAS AT JOY JUNCTION

One of Joy Junction's former staff members knows being homeless during any time of the year is devastating. "In the summer you spend your days looking for the smallest piece of shade to get some relief from the seemingly endless heat, and in the winter you begin to long for the warm sun of July."

But it is even worse at Christmas. "Being homeless at Christmas can send you down a depression tunnel that is almost impossible to pull yourself out of. You walk the streets watching decorations go up, people rushing by with bags and bags of gifts. The smell of wonderful food floods the air, and all you can do is find an alcove in an alley, keeping warm by perhaps thinking about your youth at the holiday season."

Her perspective on all this brightened when she and her children found themselves at Joy Junction during the Christmas season. "The smiles and pure joy in my children's eyes when they woke up that morning made me cry, because being here gave them a better Christmas than I could have done."

Knowing how difficult Christmas can be for our guests, we try to make it a very special time. Since I began Joy Junction in 1986, we have always had special meals and a number of seasonal activities.

We asked some of our guests their feelings about Christmas at Joy Junction.

One resident told us Joy Junction was very helpful to her during what she called her "time of weakness." She commented that she felt a lot of pressure and emotional pain during this particular period of her life, as she went from living what she called a very comfortable life to getting through days without her family. While she felt alone and abandoned, Joy Junction—recommended by a friend—has been a place of support. "I was scared and very sad. The staff has been very helpful at all times. They take the time to hear me out. Christmas at Joy Junction will be a very comfortable feeling with everyone. The prayers make it a very comfortable place. I thank God for this place."

She does feel sad during the season because she recently lost her dad, whom she called the most important man in her life. However, it's also a happy time. "Even though I may not have a real family and money to buy presents, I have made a lot of good friends that are like family. We are all in the same situation, and we love and take care of each other. The staff is great and caring. If I can't be with family, then I would choose Joy Junction to spend Christmas."

One life recovery program participant said, "It was really good. The kids got almost all the stuff they wanted. They loved Christmas dinner, and we got to be together." That same individual said a Christmas spent on the streets would have been horrible. "The kids wouldn't have got anything, and I don't know what they would have had for dinner."

Another life recovery program participant said, "My Christmas here was nothing I could have imagined. What would it have been like to spend it on the streets? Full of sadness and disappointment."

An overnight Joy Junction guest was appreciative but understandably sad. She said, "Any and all events remind me of the loss of my husband, so it's a losing proposition to try and change that fact. I enjoyed 'small niceties,' the most small thoughtful gestures that make the physical discomforts of being homeless lessened. But I see my husband everywhere and in everything." This woman said spending Christmas on the streets would have been "cold and lonely." She added, "It's very easy to lose one's perspective out there, or maybe it's reality that makes us lose our way. Nonetheless, if you don't have a social network, you can drown, and there seems to be little motivation to create one, if all you can do is think about physical discomforts. I don't believe that the joy one used to feel during the holidays will return for most of us."

Based on her own period of homelessness and talking with many others over the years, one guest's reflection on Christmas speaks for many of the homeless. She said, "The days keep moving toward Christmas, but for the homeless there is no excitement. Christmas day will be like all others, moving through the crowd faceless and nameless, looking for a little to eat, a way to stay warm, and something to numb the pain of your existence." For many on the streets, the Christmas season becomes a blur. "The only way for them to deal with past memories, knowing that they have come to the bottom, is by using alcohol and drugs to numb them from their reality."

She also said while shelters help and can be an obvious life saver, and while meals and gestures of kindness help, it is important to remember that for the homeless, "You are still eating and drinking with people you may never see again, much less sit under a tree opening gifts by a warm fire. Even though they are now warm, dry, and fed, they are still moving only through the motions of normalcy and spending the holiday with people they have no real emotional connection with. Their only common ground is that they are homeless, and they only have each other and the kindness of the shelter to look to for any emotional food."

Another guest said when you are staying at a shelter like Joy Junction where all your basic needs are taken care of, you can still feel like a huge dollop of guilt is heaped upon you. "Your mind still tumbles that you are not able to provide those basics for yourself or your family. As satisfying as it is to know you will be warm and safe on Christmas and the days to come, when you lay down on the mat or a cot that night, your mind spins with how you ended up at the mercy of a shelter."

Please say a prayer for all our city's homeless—both those who are housed and those who are unhoused. While they may not express it in a way you or I can easily understand—or be moving in a way we believe will enable them to attain their goals—all the homeless want safety, acceptance, and somewhere they can call home.

The Disappearing Diapers: A Higher Street Value Than Cocaine

During the Thanksgiving and Christmas seasons, Joy Junction is blessed with an outpouring of donations of toys, food, clothing, personal hygiene kits, and more.

One Christmas season, we had an organization donate cases and cases of diapers. While diapers may seem a pretty mundane gift to most of us, it is hard to appreciate their value until they are needed and not available. As a result, the families staying at Joy Junction felt as if Christmas had arrived early.

As things settled down (at least until the next kindhearted group of generous donors came by), we learned that a few of the shelter's single residents had taken several cases of the donated diapers. Quite understandably, we were more than a little curious and started an immediate search. We shelter between sixty and eighty children nightly with their parents, so diapers donated to Joy Junction are a precious commodity.

We found out a few of the individuals who had taken the diapers had children living off-site with family members or friends. While we were not thrilled to learn they had taken the diapers without going through the proper channels, we did understand. After all, how must these mothers feel when told by their children's caregivers that these financially unattainable items are so badly needed?

But we found out something else that floored us. One of the residents had two bundles of diapers. When we asked why she told us because there are minimal toilet facilities in downtown Albuquerque for the homeless,

168

they are in a humiliating dilemma. Because of the lack of toilets, the homeless have to disgrace themselves by urinating and defecating behind dumpsters and any other place with some privacy. It is doubly bad for females, as they must disrobe to do either.

She told us when she and other homeless individuals could not make it to a day shelter, or to Joy Junction, they could use the diapers in their jeans and then discard the waste with some dignity. When she said, "Diapers have a better street value than cocaine," this pretty much stopped us in our tracks. We had never heard of this. Humbled, we apologized to the resident for questioning her.

The lack of restrooms is a big problem, and so the homeless have learned to be creative. For public restroom facilities, many of Albuquerque's homeless use the downtown library and the Alvarado Transportation Center as their first and second choices, respectively. They have to be "sneaky" when using the Greyhound terminal. It is best to use it only when one has enough time and money to pretend one is getting a snack or looking at schedules. Even then, once they leave, they have to make sure to disappear and not hang out in front.

Some homeless people hop over fences on construction sites and use the portable toilets there. At other times, they will just "find a spot." Some Joy Junction guests say when they ask for directions to a restroom, many times they are either ignored or receive hateful responses. One person was told, "If you had a home, you would know where the bathroom is." A comment like this is so hateful it defies description.

At Joy Junction, we remember the plight of those who have no home—and no bathroom—and we always ask the Lord what we can do to help.

A Heartwarming Christmas Tale

The day before Christmas Eve was an even busier one than usual for the Joy Junction staff. Our mission, home to as many as three hundred people, including as many as eighty children, was abuzz with pre-Christmas excitement. The youngsters were very excited, like all children at this season. At least for a while, they were able to forget their homelessness and anxiously anticipate a multitude of gifts made possible by generous donors. The volunteers unloaded bags of Santa's treasures, and the children followed their parents' instruction to "open just one present today." Parents mumbled they have no idea where they will put it all.

Falling snowflakes diverted the children's attention. They came running to a manager, asking, "Can you call Dr. Reynalds? Please." Why did the youngsters want them to call me? The manager tried explaining I was very busy.

The kids insisted. "Ask him if we can build a snowman." "Does he like snowball fights?" "Will he let [kitchen manager] Mike make us snow ice cream?" The manager laughed and promised he would email their requests to my ever-active BlackBerry and return with an answer should we actually get enough snow to scoop up.

This was not what the kids wanted to hear. Slightly annoyed, they wandered off with a parting comment, "You better remember. We are gonna ask him. He likes us." As the manager watched the children make their way to a Christmas activity, he was reminded about the true meaning of Christmas and why we give gifts.

Another one was touched when she heard the kids talk about how the Lord would understand their dilemma and phone the good Dr. Reynalds.

One of our managers said, "I remember flashes of my Christmases prior to Joy Junction. But I never felt love or the true spirit of Christmas until I came here. Someday I will live in a dwelling away from the loving land of Joy Junction. Who knew this ground could be so blessed or beautiful? But I hope God will call Dr. Reynalds every year and remind him to invite me home for the holidays."

I appreciate the tireless efforts of our staff. Working at Joy Junction is so much more than a job. It is a calling. We thank our Lord for his faithfulness, and we thank our donors for supporting us. Without them, we could not share the love of Jesus with the ever-increasing number of people in need.

Comments From Some Facebook Friends

I asked some of our Facebook friends what they thought it would be like being homeless for Christmas

One woman said she wouldn't know what to think. She wrote, "I have never been homeless, and I would not know the feeling. Each day I travel to work I see homeless people . . . and I deeply feel so sad. Each morning I pray with my child for others."

Homelessness would be "awful," another person said.

"I might not have everything, but I have a warm home and plenty of food to eat! My heart truly goes out to those that don't have their basic needs met! God bless you all at Joy Junction for making this wicked world we live in a better place."

Someone else said it would be "devastating" to be homeless, while another person commented that while her mom was homeless for the last three Christmases, that has all changed. She continued, "I am so happy that she is blessed to be clean sober and will have a warm home this Christmas. I wish no one had to experience this at any time during the year."

Joy Junction is all about ending hunger and homelessness, one meal and one life at a time. We'd like all of our guests to experience future Christmases in their own homes. However, until that happens, we're focusing on giving on making Christmas at Joy Junction the best it can possibly be.

Food for Thought

Francis Schaeffer said, "Biblical orthodoxy without compassion is surely the ugliest thing in the world." Do you agree with him?

Imagine you are homeless during Christmas. What would you do? Where would you go?

AN INCREDIBLE
JOURNEY

n the 2009 inaugural edition of Joy Junction's *Good News Gazette,* we mentioned a desire to run a lunch wagon that would be filled with coffee, soup, sandwiches, and other food with which we could bless the homeless. The plan was for the wagon to visit areas frequented by the homeless and provide a lifeline in the form of food, drink, and prayer. This lifeline of hope would let those using its services know someone cares. And it might even save a life—or more.

As mentioned earlier, a few days later, I received an e-mail from Vic Jury, a longtime friend of Joy Junction and CEO of Summit Electric Supply. He said he had gone online and found something on eBay that may work for us. I took a look and was immediately excited. The vehicle looked like it was everything we needed to make our vision a reality.

The problem was the vehicle was in Florida's West Palm Beach. I thought and prayed and sensed the Lord wanted me to personally go and pick it up. I mentioned this to the donor who immediately responded that if I was sure I wanted to do this, he would pay for my airline ticket. What a wonderful blessing!

A few days later, along with Terry, a former employee from Joy Junction's corporate office who offered to come along with me, we set off. Those three days were truly a whirlwind of activity but also provided an opportunity for me to reflect on the Lord's goodness—both to me personally and to Joy Junction.

Day I: The Journey Begins

Sleep eluded me for much of the night as I lay there tossing and turning, waiting for the alarm to go off at 4:45 a.m. to signal the time to get up and catch the 7:10 plane for Florida.

I stumbled out of bed, took two aspirin to ward off the painful rumblings of an approaching headache, forsook my usual chai latte, and turned on the shower.

After a much quicker than usual trip to the airport down a relatively deserted road, I arrived at a packed airline ticket counter where I met Terry.

There was a quick trip through security and then time for a quick stop for chai (and a piece of ham and green chili quiche). The lady serving me the chai looked at me and said, "Oh, I didn't think you'd have time to travel."

A little taken aback, I answered, "I'm on the way to pick up a donation for Joy Junction—a lunch wagon."

"Oh," she said. That was it, other than a comment that my quiche would be at the microwave. Oh, the joys of being known!

We made our way to the line for the plane. The adventure was beginning. Our plan was to get to West Palm Beach to pick up the lunch wagon and drive it the five or six hours north to Tallahassee before we stopped for the night.

Boarding the plane, I told a cheery Southwest flight attendant I was hoping for lots of jokes.

"Maybe singing," he said with a smile.

A few minutes later, we were airborne for the first leg of our journey, which would take us through Houston and Tampa on our way to West Palm Beach.

The flight was smooth and uneventful, but toward the end I was thinking the flight attendant had let me down on his promise to sing. Just then, he burst into song, singing something like, "We love you, you love us, and we're much faster than a bus. Marry one of us, and you'll fly free."

I love Southwest Airlines humor! It continued just prior to the next leg of the flight, with one of the crew members asking people to hurry up and get all the formalities disposed of so we could take off. He said his wife had just called, and his mother-in-law was getting through security. He wanted the plane in the air before she made it, he said. Most of the passengers laughed.

The Houston–Tampa leg of our trip was pretty smooth, and I passed the time by reading a captivating, eye-opening, and horrifying book by Nick Reding titled *Methland: The Death and Life of an American Small Town*. After a quick layover in Tampa and time to take care of some e-mails and phone calls, we boarded another plane for West Palm Beach. Making my way up the aisle, I couldn't help but overhear hear one side of a conversation. Speaking on his cell phone rather loudly, a man was saying, "I'm fifty-two, I don't do drugs, and I don't want kids."

Hmm, I thought. *Now we've got that taken care of, tell me how you really feel.* I wondered about the other half of that conversation.

The flight from Tampa to West Palm Beach was short and uneventful, and about forty-five minutes or so later, we touched down. The humidity hung in the air even in the air-conditioned airport. While I love mountains and the ocean, humidity is definitely not for me.

Outside the airport where a dealership employee was waiting to give us a ride to the truck, we were assaulted by even worse humidity. We arrived at the dealership a few minutes later and saw the beautiful lunch wagon. We were introduced to the general manager, a man not shy about sharing his faith, who asked us about Joy Junction and how I began the shelter over two decades earlier. When I shared with him what the lunch truck would be used for, he seemed delighted. I think he initially believed we would be selling food as a profit-making enterprise. His mouth dropped when I told him what we had in mind.

After signing all the papers necessary to transfer ownership of the lunch truck to Joy Junction, we were on our way. We prayed, asking for the Lord's blessing, and Terry started driving what the dealership staff called our "Lunch Mobile 747."

As we drove, we tuned in to a variety of country music stations (each fading out of range quickly) to make sure we stayed alert and awake. In a couple of hours we pulled into a rest stop area for some food. Terry had a wrap, and I somehow ended up with another piece of ham quiche—but minus the green chili. This wasn't New Mexico.

We had another couple of hours before reaching Tallahassee. Terry continued driving, for which I was grateful. This gave me the opportunity to write as we moved down the road. Even while sitting in the "747" and rolling toward our hotel, ideas were beginning to swirl in my mind about how we could best bless the homeless with our new acquisition. We already had a staff member who was very interested in being involved in the lunch truck operation. I was pumped about this new ministry!

We continued driving, and I kept on answering e-mails and writing. I also checked on some of the early Albuquerque municipal election results by going to Facebook. My life without Facebook and BlackBerry? Did I even have one?

Within about fifty miles of our hotel, I was just worn out. I felt grimy, my legs were aching, my back hurt, and I just wanted rest. How grateful I was for a motel room, a clean bed, and a place to stay. My thoughts went to why we were doing this cross-country jaunt in the first place: to make living easier for the homeless and perhaps even save people's lives by giving them food and water.

How thankful I was for this wonderful donor who had purchased the vehicle for our use and for the Lord who continues sustaining this amazing ministry.

A few minutes after we pulled into our motel and checked in, I thanked the Lord for his goodness and collapsed into bed!

Day 2: The Incredible Journey Continues

It was 9:30 a.m. in Florida—7:30 back home—and time to get on the road. Our marathon trek in the 747 Lunch Wagon continued on to Dallas.

Note to the TSA folks: if you unscrew liquids in my suitcase, would you please screw the cap back on so they don't spill all over my clothes and everything else? Thanks!

As I stepped out of the hotel, it was so humid my glasses fogged up. This was just so not me. I couldn't wait for Albuquerque!

A chai latte and a sausage piadina would have to suffice for now. I made my way back to the lunch wagon through the parking lot. It would be next to impossible to miss this beautiful vehicle, so I didn't have to wander directionally challenged around the parking lot in search of my little Pontiac Vibe.

After asking the Lord's blessing on the day and our travel, we took off, Terry behind the wheel and me beside him, e-mailing and taking care of JJ business from the BlackBerry—my mobile office! As I did so, I was listening to the words of the song "Live Like You're Dying." This country tune had an obvious biblical theme. How would we change the way we live if we knew we only had a short time left? I can speak only for myself, but I think there might be some significant changes.

We had an uneventful morning and pulled into a Chick-fil-A for a quick lunch before making our way over to Jackson, Mississippi, where we stopped to feed the 747. After we pulled into a gas station with heavily barred windows, my attempts to pay at the pump were met with a computer-generated message telling me to see the attendant. I did just that, but when I offered him a credit card, he said somewhat tersely, "We don't take no credit cards." We didn't stop to inquire further. We just thanked him and went a few hundred feet across the street to a station that did.

Our next stop was for coffee and a couple of other small purchases. I used my Visa debit card and was very surprised when it was denied.

A call a few minutes later to my credit union revealed that the credit function of the debit card had been uniformly disabled for all members in about six states due to data that had been compromised somewhere and somehow earlier that year. Fortunately, I had an alternative method of payment. While I later learned the debit function still worked, it took a call to the credit union to find that out. Another on-the-road adventure.

We plowed on, driving I-20 west to Dallas. Somewhere west of Shreveport and about 170 miles east of Dallas, we stopped for a fast-food supper. We didn't want to stray too far off the highway, and as a friend told me, "Fine dining off the highway is an oxymoron!" My buffalo wings with honey mustard sauce, a small order of fries, and a tiny cup of coffee testified to how true that was. A few minutes later, we were on our way. Dallas, here we come! What a whirlwind trip this was. As usual, my BlackBerry kept me in touch with everything and everyone.

Close to our hotel and very tired, Terry and I were encouraged to see the Soulman's Barbeque Restaurant with a Jesus is Lord sign.

A few minutes later, with the help of the GPS on the BlackBerry, we pulled into our hotel. The good Lord had given us another day to serve him before collapsing into bed.

Day 3: The Incredible Journey Concludes

The third day of a road trip needs to begin with two things: prayer and a visit to Starbucks. While talking to the barista, I said I was on the way home to Albuquerque. Another employee overheard me and said she loved Hatch green chili. She'd never been to New Mexico, but friends regularly sent her chili from there. I left with my chai, happy to have reminded her of New Mexico. Maybe I made her day a bit better.

Terry and I sharing the driving, and I e-mailed prolifically when not behind the wheel. Running Joy Junction is a never-ending job, even in the cab of a 747 lunch wagon, and it is definitely never boring.

Later in the afternoon we arrived in Amarillo. It would be hard not to pay a visit to the Big Texan, home of the free seventy-two-ounce steak—free, that is, if you are able to devour the gargantuan slice of meat and sides in an hour or less. I'd been there a number of times, but Terry had never visited. He had a much-smaller-than-seventy-two-ounce steak, and I tried a heart-stopping, artery-clogging chicken fried steak. Both the food and the service were excellent.

Bone-chilling temperatures assaulted us when we left the restaurant, which made me thank the Lord for the safety of a warm truck and the promise of a warm and safe house and a comfortable bed when the trip was finished. I was unaware of the homeless situation in Amarillo, but I breathed a quick prayer for the Lord's blessing and protection for those homeless souls who, for whatever reason, would have no place to stay that night.

We fed the 747 and started off on the last leg of our long and tiring journey and were in New Mexico only a short while later. And we were there with a food truck—a very tangible lifeline for the homeless. It was so good to be home again and enjoy the beautiful sunset as we got closer to Albuquerque. I so much appreciate New Mexico where I have spent more than half of my life.

Food for Thought

Close to forty major cities across the United States have instituted food-sharing restrictions, reasoning the homeless will go away by cutting off food sources. Do you agree with this attitude? What do you think of cities curtailing certain works of mercy?

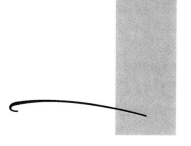

LOVE AND HELP OR ANGER, RIDICULE, AND COMPLAINTS: YOU CHOOSE

Actress from Down Under Thinks New Mexico Has a "Gummy" Problem

Along with Tina Fey, Australian actress Margot Robbie was on a recent edition of The Late Show with Stephen Colbert promoting the movie *Whiskey Tango Foxtrot*, released in early 2016. The movie is set in Afghanistan and was filmed in 2015 in New Mexico. Fey asked Colbert whether he'd been to New Mexico. He said no, and Robbie jumped in with what she thought was a funny quip.

"Lots of missing teeth," said Robbie.

The remark drew a lot of laughter from Fey and the audience, but, along with many others, I was not amused.

Robbie's remark was hurtful. While she wasn't referring specifically to the homeless, it struck a chord with me because the homeless—for a variety of reasons—often lack teeth. Their gummy situation just serves to further exacerbate the often overwhelming sense of inadequacy and lack of self-confidence they already feel.

I asked my staff to find a few of our guests without teeth and see what they felt about Robbie's thoughtless statement.

One person said, "I feel labeled, judged, and categorized without my teeth. Because of my own experience of bad teeth in the past, I feel defined by my teeth or lack thereof. I feel insulted and ashamed. I had all of my teeth pulled at a young age due to genetics and poor choices. [Robbie's] comment in my opinion, suggests that the state of New Mexico is looked down upon, and is in poverty and is full of addicts. I feel if the lack of teeth is that much of a concern, then perhaps the actress can look into contributing a solution instead of criticizing and labeling the state."

Another person said that lacking teeth results in a feeling of shame, not being able to smile and an avoidance of conversations. "It's (also) hard not having teeth to chew my food. Medically, it's very unhealthy for me. If I had full set of teeth, my morale would be much better. I would smile more and I would be able to chew my food without swallowing it whole."

Another person we spoke to doesn't smile or laugh around people because people stare at her mouth. "I know, because I stare at people's mouths, too. I would love to have a full set of teeth so I can smile, laugh and talk more often," that individual added. "I would love to have my picture taken and show people that I love to be around them.

And what about Robbie? "I wish (she) didn't say what she did. She doesn't know that pain I feel about not having teeth. It wasn't very nice of her."

Another person wrote, "I'm personally missing all of my teeth and have to wear dentures. It's not because of drugs, but from an abusive relationship." Happily, she said, "I now have a husband that assures me that I'm beautiful with or without teeth . . . It's disappointing and sad that people can't seem to see past a set of teeth. It's a good thing that my self-esteem doesn't depend on people like [Robbie]."

I asked some of our Joy Junction Facebook fans what they thought about Robbie's comments. They weren't very complimentary.

Samantha said having a pretty face doesn't necessarily mean pretty on the inside. She added, "My Nana taught me that growing up. 'Be pretty on the inside, and you'll be pretty on the outside, but if you're ugly on the inside it will come out and show itself.' My Nana was from Mississippi; she always had something good like that!"

Richard suggested, "Someone who cares about Margo Robbie might offer her a tour of the states' better neighborhoods. A complete lack of class."

Becky commented, "Too bad her attempt at comedy is at the expense of those not there to defend themselves, or make a 'funny' comment back about her lack of comedic talent or good manners."

William said that while the comment was made in the context of a comedy show, "It reveals how shallow people can be. I'm sure she regrets making the comment."

Stefanie called her comment a disappointment. "How quick she forgets that this state offers a lot to bring movies here that pay her."

Cynthia encouraged an attitude of humility like Jesus. She concluded by saying that we shouldn't "poke fun at the less fortunate. Tomorrow is not promised to any of us. Let us walk in the Love of Jesus our Savior."

Amen, Cynthia. Sadly, we seem to live in a culture where it's seemingly acceptable for almost anything to be said. Having cable news on in the background today while I worked was probably a mistake. I tuned in to hear "news," but what I ended up getting for the most part was often angry, hate-filled punditry, about how the "other side" was wrong.

I confess I wondered how much of the animus and angst I heard was genuine, or whether some sprang from a desire to get ratings. Easy-to-understand issues, which can be separated by the media into two opposing and angry sides, often do very well in the ratings. It makes it easy for the talking heads to play to the crowds. That translates into higher advertising revenues for the network and a longer and possibly more lucrative contract for the "expert" commentator.

What Would You Do if This Was Your Last Day on Earth?

That question got me thinking from an eternal perspective. I posted these questions on a couple of our Facebook pages—both Joy Junction's and mine. "If this was our last day on earth, what would they say about us the day after? What would our tombstone read? Would we be known as critics of the homeless or lovers of the needy? Would we be Jesus people, or critics of society? Do we want to be known for what we are against? What defines us?"

I received only a few responses to my Facebook question, but they were good ones. Ann wrote she believes our actions define us. "Words mean nothing without an action to back them up. I bring up God in every conversation I have, with every person I meet, every chance I get. I share my homeless story and my never ending faith in knowing that God had a purpose for me no matter where my journey has led."

Ann said she would even feed a hungry person if she hadn't yet eaten. She continued, "I will give up my coat, my socks and shoes, my prepaid phone, or anything else I could help with if it meant even one person could have a better day today than they did yesterday."

Those are pretty powerful words—and actions. Ann is a disabled former guest of Joy Junction who loves to tell people about the blessings and love of God. "My words were a promise I made years ago when I left JJ and said that I would pay it forward. I have tried to do that every day. In return, God has blessed me in too many ways to count."

Helen Ann said doing the best we can is pleasing to God. She said doing the scriptural works of mercy covers everything. "Feed the hungry, clothe the naked, visit the sick, visit or pray for those who are in prison, give drink to the thirsty, shelter the homeless, and bury the dead. If we do this it shows action speaks louder than words, and Jesus will bless us and be very happy and pleased."

Tosie said doing good deeds with a happy heart is pleasing to God. She added, "If we get praise for our good deeds on earth we might not get rewarded in heaven. It's good if we do good that others on earth never know about. Then they will give the thanks only to God."

The responses of these three people are full of wisdom. Here is what I hear in their words: "Despite what you have or how you are feeling, help others and do so cheerfully and quietly. As a result, people will give the glory to God." None of these three people are complaining or blaming. They are just going quietly about their daily business and making a difference. They are lovers, not haters.

What characteristic will most closely define you when it comes time for your epitaph or obituary? It is worth thinking about, because one day the words best describing the years we have spent on earth will be written. Nobody will leave this world alive, but all of us can play a major part in forming our legacy and the way people remember us. What will your epitaph say?

Albuquerque's Smelliest Problem

A story by KOB-TV 4 in Albuquerque reported that some downtown business owners are just plain fed up. They say while homeless people come to eat at the Albuquerque Rescue Mission, once the facility closes its doors there is no place for the homeless to use the restroom. So they just do so in alleyways or on the side of buildings.

On a trip through downtown Albuquerque on a warm Saturday evening, I saw about thirty or so people outside the mission in a well-lit area, either sleeping or preparing to sack out for the night. While there was a little movement, everything looked pretty calm. Just a few hundred yards away from the mission where a number of homeless people had been "setting up camp" for a while, everything was deserted. It looked as if some of the same individuals had just moved a short distance northeast to a more secluded area under a nearby overpass.

Having worked with New Mexico's homeless for over thirty years, I sympathize with the business owners' concerns. Yet there is no quick fix. It is unfair to blame the Albuquerque Rescue Mission and expect the City of Albuquerque to come up with an overnight answer. That just isn't going to happen.

What is the answer? I suggest beginning with a community conversation among the business owners (both those affected and citywide), the Albuquerque Rescue Mission, and the City of Albuquerque. Also important to a solution and an integral part of the initial discussion would be an understanding of exactly who the homeless are and why some well-meaning missions are unable to help them. We've described some of the many people we meet to illustrate there are many reasons why people are homeless. One size does not fit all.

While Joy Junction is in the South Valley and thus far removed from the concentration of other assistance for the homeless, our van services extend to downtown Albuquerque. We also make regular patrols through downtown during the night to see if anyone there wants a place to stay and to drop off sack lunches and bottled water.

Who are some of the people causing the current wave of concern? Based on both my own personal observation and talks with our staff, they are four types of people. First, they include those who would like a place to stay if offered, but are unable to access one because all the shelters (as well as Joy Junction) are full. Second, some are also people with mental health challenges who are unable to be around the usually large number of people in a shelter. Third, some are individuals with a history of violence and drug dealers who try to blend in with the homeless. On top of that, fourth, there are those in the throes of an active drug or alcohol addiction. Before you write them off, consider this question. What was going on in someone's life to drive them to try finding a refuge for their pain in illegal drugs or the inappropriate use of alcohol?

To make things harder, Metropolitan Assessment and Treatment Services—MATS—the local detox (and an excellent facility), won't service anyone with a warrant. That is an obvious issue, because any number of homeless individuals can get a summons to appear in court for, say, panhandling. And if they fail to appear in court, a warrant is issued for their failure to appear. Who wants a trip to jail to get off your addiction? So this question is more complicated than might be imagined.

I wondered what Facebook friends and fans thought could be done. Lynda suggested that homeless services "be spread around a little." However, she had it right when she speculated, "I'm sure all hell would break loose if someone dared to try and open a facility in upper-middle to upper-class neighborhoods of the Northeast Heights or the Taylor Ranch area." Zoning regulations and neighborhood opposition make it very difficult—almost impossible—to start new missions centers or feeding centers. The old acronym NIMBY comes to mind: not in my back yard! Everyone agrees something should be done, but the solution shouldn't be close to them.

I thought Rachel had a good point in saying her guess is half of the businesses complaining only offer a restroom for their customers. She continued, "If you don't want them defecating around your business, how about offering a restroom for them? You keep an eye out so there are no issues (drug violence and so on), and that problem is solved— sorta—rather than putting the responsibility all on the city."

She added that while these business owners would say that would be bad for business, perhaps there is another side to that argument. "Showing compassion versus hostility would be a great virtue in a business owner."

The KOB reporter asked a city official why the city just couldn't just put up a couple of porta-potties. The official answer was that it could "add to the problem." Presumably, he was thinking of the same answer a former city official gave years ago when I suggested porta-potties, and he answered they can encourage prostitution and drug use/dealing.

Donna said that despite problems with public restrooms, they should still be provided. "Perhaps some of the more reliable, responsible people could be in charge of cleaning and maintenance, which would give a sense of purpose and worth."

The restrooms idea is a good one, but I don't think having the homeless provide cleaning services would work. I like what someone else said, that perhaps the only solution, or even the best solution at the moment, is to have a city crew clean them up in shifts.

But Donna had it right when she wrote, "There are never simple straightforward answers because the problem itself is neither simple nor straightforward. But, that shouldn't mean we give up and wash our hands. It means we should dig deeper and think outside the box. During these times of hardship for everyone, I think we need to dig deeper inside ourselves as well."

Albuquerque's smelliest problem is a multifaceted issue. It will only be alleviated when our entire community takes on the responsibility for the less fortunate among us and communicates instead of blames and ignores.

Food for Thought

"Despite what you have or how you are feeling, help others and do so cheerfully and quietly. As a result people will give the glory to God." Those words come from some of the homeless people we have met. Can you put the idea they are expressing in your own words?

What characteristic will most closely define you when it comes time for your epitaph or obituary?

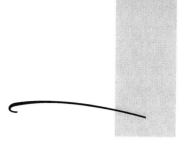

WHO IS SAYING BAD THINGS ABOUT THE HOMELESS?

You would be surprised who has bad words to say about the homeless. We have been blessed and honored beyond adequate words by some of the people who have felt moved to support Joy Junction by fundraising contributions, donations of food and supplies, and donations of time. I hope they have felt useful and valued, because they are.

To be frank, though, those who have not had exposure to homeless people or a homeless ministry sometimes have misconceptions that make me sad.

Mixing Religion with Delivery of Services

I was flabbergasted to hear about the head of a homeless agency thinking it is "immoral" to mix religion with delivery of services to the homeless. Maybe he or his clients have had bad experiences with those who combine religion with helping the homeless. If that is the case, it is very sad, because the gospel is supposed to be good news. At Joy Junction, a faith-based ministry, we think sharing Jesus kindly and compassionately with our guests is essential. Why do we feel so strongly about that message? It is because my experience working with New Mexico's homeless for over thirty years teaches me that people often fall into drug abuse and an inappropriate use of alcohol to escape the emotional pain and despair characterizing their lives. While regularly working with medical and mental health professionals, Joy Junction offers a relationship with Jesus Christ as the cornerstone on which to build a fully recovered life. We believe that to do otherwise would be "immoral."

To find out if there are people who agree about sharing the gospel when helping the homeless with food and shelter, I asked some of our Facebook friends. Is it immoral to mix religion with delivery of services to the homeless? Is it immoral not to? They were quick to respond.

Rita was very much in favor of sharing the gospel while helping the homeless. She said, "I am a graduate of Joy Junction. It is an establishment that helped me in so many ways. And having a devotional in the mornings helped set the path for a new day."

Angel said, "It is essential and very much needed. Your ministry is wonderful not only for the homeless but for those who are not homeless. If only more people followed your example."

Charles could see no other way of offering hope to the homeless outside of sharing the message of Christ. He said Jesus gives hope to those who feel they have none. He added, "Keep up the good work, Joy Junction. And when someone tells you to not mix religious beliefs with helping someone, or when they tell you to turn your shirt inside out, remember Romans 1:16: 'For I am not ashamed of the gospel, because it is the power of God that brings salvation to everyone who believes.'"

Andrea commented, "I'm Jewish, so the way I see it, your Savior was a Jew—so it's all fine. Besides, if someone doesn't want to hear the preaching, they will tell you. I give to various food banks and to Joy Junction. The bottom line is *tzedakah* (charity). Give to those less fortunate than yourself."

I like what Joel said. "I'm not a big fan of anyone pushing any religion; however, at Joy Junction you do it with taste and class. You do not try to ram it down anyone's throat like some other groups. I may not believe in the same God that you do, but when someone tells me 'God bless,' I don't get insulted by it. I say 'Thank you,' and then go about my day."

Paula also had encouraging words. She wrote that while she believes in "live and let live," as long as no one is being hurt, "I firmly believe in God, and that's what makes me the strong, compassionate, and giving person I am. I appreciate your organization, and I am glad to see you doing all you do. If you want to praise our Lord, I stand behind you one hundred and ten percent."

Destiny said she was okay with sharing Jesus with our guests so long as food or services are not denied to those who reject religion or our Christian outlook on it. Helping those in need should be just that, without pushing your agenda on them. I love the work Joy Junction does, though, and I donate to them all the time."

I appreciate everyone who responded. A question for those who do not believe in sharing the gospel when assisting the homeless, is this: What other form of real encouragement is there for a homeless and hungry person after the basic human needs have been cared for?

The following are some anecdotes that illustrate some of the negative comments homeless people experience about the public's perception of them.

Johnny: "We Are Vapors"

It's hard enough being homeless. When you're robbed of the possessions you have and the few dollars you might get for a day's labor, it just adds insult to injury. Sadly, that happens all the time. When our staff first heard about these incidents, we assumed it was random street violence. But then we heard non-homeless individuals driving, in some cases, reasonably nice vehicles were carrying out these attacks.

With that in mind, we investigated with a weeklong information scavenger hunt. Many of our Joy Junction staff have lived among and worked with the homeless population for many years and have seen them being treated with disdain, disrespect, and cruelty. But being targets of hate crimes?

When we started digging into these crimes, which apparently happen quite frequently on the streets of downtown Albuquerque, every victim we spoke with said the perpetrator made some comment like "You're homeless anyway. It's not like you have to pay rent with this money." This made our hearts skip as we walked back to the van, feeling rage we hadn't felt in years."

Johnny has lived on the streets for close to thirty years. We don't know his exact age, but he is probably in his late eighties. He is a gentle and calm spirit who cannot function in mainstream society. He asks for little, and to those who live around him, he gives all.

We made our way into the alley where Johnny has his pop-up house and we tapped on the side. He appeared and invited us in. To our surprise, he was eating a hamburger, a meal he was appearing to relish. He caught our glance and smiled, explaining that sometimes the restaurant nearby would let him sweep the parking lot for a meal. One of our team members asked Johnny if we could talk to him while he ate. He said, "Of course."

Johnny had heard of these crimes that seemed to be multiplying, and he said they were nothing new. He said he had never been a victim; he was "the wrong homeless class to be rolled by them."

The wrong homeless class? We said, "Johnny, homeless is homeless." He said, 'No. Homeless is not homeless.'"

He told us there are three "classes" of homeless people. "There are the homeless that Joy Junction primarily serves," Johnny said. "They have fallen on hard times, have abuse problems, or are 'system homeless.' Their parents never really stood on solid ground, nor their parents before them, so they were never given the skills to keep a job, pay rent, car payments and do all the other things necessary for life."

Johnny said there are also what he called "warrior" homeless. "They're in small-time drug sales, drink a lot, and are in and out of jail. Some are gang members. They want to stay under law enforcement radar."

Then there are "street homeless." Johnny said, "That is me. Now don't get me wrong. I have been known to have whisky to help keep this old body warm and will say here and now I will use it again, but only when available."

He smiled and continued. "My people don't come out in the day, and at night we are vapors, the shadow you thought you might have seen. I don't panhandle, and I don't steal. I sweep here for food and there for smokes. I receive social security and a little from the veterans. It pays for my medication and propane for my stove. I walk to Tingley Beach and fish when I get hungry for my mama's fish and chips. My class of homeless does not exist."

Johnny said people who are just getting by hate the sort of homeless served by Joy Junction. He said, "These rolls are hate crimes. The people who function every day through a shelter are tagged by those who just hocked their car title to pay the rent or buy food. They know your homeless will be fed and pay nothing to sleep warm and take a hot shower. They feel your homeless people have more, and it is all given to them."

We told Johnny that when he said his class of homeless did not exist he was wrong. We told him he did exist and that he was a very special soul.

The misconceptions about the homeless—even among the homeless themselves—are always troubling. As the sun came up and we made our way back to Joy Junction, we encountered a man at a convenience store who recognized us from the shelter. He asked how we could sleep with a bunch of dirty bums.

I wish those who see us downtown or anywhere, flying a sign or sitting on the corner waiting for the day to go by, would come to Joy Junction and take a tour before they judge us or the people we serve. I wish they would see what our reality is.

At Joy Junction the lights come on at six o'clock in the morning, and there is *no* snooze button to hit for just fifteen more minutes. There is no stretching and wandering to the kitchen for a cup of coffee in your robe. With their daily struggles, many of our residents see no hope. Suffering the sort of vicious attacks we have been seeing recently in Albuquerque, which I really believe are hate crimes, can be the final indignity.

Complaints About Crab Legs with Food Stamps? Hmmm . . .

If you have teenagers, it probably won't be long after denying a request for an extended curfew or the latest, expensive name-brand fashion that you hear the words from your indignant youngster: "Everyone's doing it."

Some careful parental investigation soon shows that while some are "doing it," that by no means extends to "everyone." Let me describe a recent event and some comments that disseminate what I think are erroneous conceptions about how the poor and hungry survive on food stamps and government programs.

A lawmaker said he was getting continual complaints from "broken-hearted" working people who have noticed purchases of extravagant foods that they, the taxpayers, cannot afford. He commented that it's not a bad idea to cut nearly two million people off the Supplemental Nutrition Assistance Program (SNAP).

So how do poor, hungry, and homeless people feel about these allegations? One Albuquerque resident who used to receive food stamps told me via Facebook, "Not everyone buys food that way. When I had food stamps I bought what was cheap to make it last the whole month. I love *how* many people think everyone does this." The individual, a former front-end manager at Walmart, continued, "I did see some customers doing this, but the majority of people going through the registers were buying cheap food and getting cookies for their kids, but kids deserve to have treats. The few will ruin it for the people who struggle every day."

Some Joy Junction guests had strong opinions. One defended the purchase of an occasionally "extravagant" meal. "[Food stamp recipients] should not be expected to [continuously] eat ramen noodles, beans, rice, tortillas, and the like . . . just because of their low income. Low income persons are people, too, and should have that option of having a nice meal once in a while, especially if they have budgeted their assistance to accommodate their wants and needs."

I have noticed a sober reality about the increase, not just in homelessness, but also in hunger in the Albuquerque area. I see an increased number of people looking for help the last two weeks of the month.

That's because food stamps don't usually last four weeks. Ideally, they should be supplemented by cash—if you have any! We hear frequent stories of people whose only food is what they receive from our Lifeline of Hope. We typically provide a hot meal and a sack lunch for later.

So is it okay to cut the food stamp program? I have serious issues with this reasoning. I don't doubt people have seen some food stamp recipients buying what the public might consider to be "inappropriate" foods. The question is, how many have they seen and how often? Do their checkout line observations mean anything in the context of a move to make serious cuts to a national food assistance program?

Anecdotal evidence is insufficient. References to a quantifiable study by the lawmaker would be much more helpful.

I heard another troubling comment from a person who was questioning the hunger issue in America. He said because we have an obesity problem, then perhaps the need isn't as bad as we've been told. It disappointed me that the person did not understand it's cheaper to buy a high-fat, high-calorie burger, fries, and coke (or similar) than a good salad or something else appropriately healthy.

Food Envy

We regularly post stories about our residents and activities on our website, www.joyjunction.org, and on our Facebook page. This simple and routine post drew a surprising response. The words read, "Our guests enjoyed posole with beef, chili and a tortilla topped off with ice cream (not together!). Was your lunch as good?"

I really didn't think much about what I'd written after I sent the update from my BlackBerry. For some time, we've been posting pictures of a couple of the three meals we serve daily at Joy Junction. Friends and fans seem to like the pictures, and I have thought letting supporters know regularly what sort of meals we serve to the hungry and homeless makes them feel more a part of our ministry and shows them what sort of meals their donations provide.

But the recent posting I mentioned above turned out to be a bit different. It wasn't long after putting the post on Facebook that I received a shocking response. The woman wrote, "You might want to stop posting pictures of the food at your homeless shelter. It can get a little old seeing homeless people eating better than the rest of us."

After reading this, my heart rate went up a little. I became momentarily upset with the post writer, but then the emotion changed to sadness. After all, what sort of person would write something like this?

It seemed like a case of "food envy." That's what KOB-TV's Caleb James titled his piece on the incident, which aired the same evening.

Once my heart rate returned to its normal level I toyed briefly with not responding, but after breathing a quick prayer, I came up with these words: "Okay, your input is needed and appreciated. After seeing this meal picture, a Facebook friend wrote that 'It gets a little old seeing homeless people eating better than the rest of us.' She suggested we might want to quit these kinds of food pictures. What do you say? Albuquerqueans and businesses make this possible!"

The words seemed just right. After all, Joy Junction's Facebook and other social media pages are for our friends, fans and followers. They're not for me, so why not ask them what they thought? And it didn't take long for the comments to start pouring in. They were overwhelmingly in favor of us continuing to post the pictures.

Manny wrote that the woman sounded like she has some sort of a complex. He continued, "What are we supposed to feed the homeless and needy? Cold baloney sandwiches with mayonnaise and a half dried up apple? Anyone who thinks that way needs to check their heart and their mind too. Shameful, very shameful."

Gina said she couldn't believe that somebody actually wrote those words. "Do they not know this is maybe their only meal that day or week, or their last meal, so why not make it great and appealing. Why shouldn't homeless be given something decent?" She went on to comment that what we post helps make people more aware of the plight faced by the homeless and how they can get involved. As she explained, "Most of us do have the means to eat decent meals even if we do spend it on cell phones, cable, Internet, and other things we don't need. Sending prayers for our homeless and for the people who don't understand."

Marvin seemed to sum up the conversation. "People who think the same way the complaining writer does do not understand the degradation of homelessness and that they are one thousand times better off than a person without a place to call home." He had a challenge for them. "Please find it in your heart to try and understand that people deserve to feel human. Go to Joy Junction and give some time, so that you might begin to be able to feel your heart beat."

Marvin, I couldn't agree more. And yes, we plan to keep on posting meal pictures!

Food for Thought

How do you feel about the homeless? Do you think they have special privileges we taxpayers, homeowners, and other people who have a place to call home do not have?

Have you ever thought of Jesus being homeless? He said he was: "Foxes have dens and birds have nests, but the Son of Man has no place to lay his head" (Matt. 8:20 and Luke 9:58).

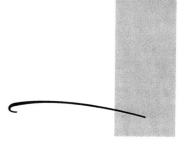

DAYS AND NIGHTS ON ALBUQUERQUE STREETS

t had been a rough day physically. I didn't feel well, but I figured one surefire way to take my mind off a stomachache was to focus on the needs of others. That evening I would encounter many others during a Joy Junction street outreach. On the way to downtown Albuquerque, my stomach was doing a dance, so I stopped off at a convenience store to get Pepto-Bismol. Maybe two small orders of fried clams earlier on in the day (comfort food for me) hadn't been the best choice!

It was seventy-nine degrees as I pulled into our downtown parking lot just before nine at night. The van was loaded with sack lunches and water.

At our first location we found a number of people, including one man who exhibited many of the characteristics of mental illness. We gave him and a handful of other people sack lunches and drove south a bit.

We arrived at our next stop, where we found seven men again unable to find shelter for the night. One man had fashioned a makeshift bed out of a plastic garbage bag he found on the street. Another guy put an empty soup box under his head, while someone else used an old jacket for a blanket. No one else out there had covers or mats. They propped themselves against the wall and gazed at us plaintively. Some of the men slept with their shoes under their heads. This is a theft prevention measure and is usually effective. If one has shoes of the slip-on variety, sleepers wouldn't wake up if someone pulled them off while they were sleeping.

As we drove on, I reflected, "Downtown Albuquerque on the weekend—nothing but trouble!" We stopped at an abandoned building where a couple of nights before we spotted an inebriated pair sleeping. No one was there this time, and no signs of their earlier presence remained, so we stopped to get coffee.

We moved onto the heart of downtown Albuquerque and fed about a half dozen people. One guy admitted he was homeless but said he didn't need a place to stay because he had a place to camp. He looked very scared, a potential victim waiting to be taken advantage of. That reminded me how I would feel if I suddenly became homeless again. We talked about trying to find him again to see if we could help, but unfortunately we weren't able to do so.

We drove over to the Fourth Street "mall," apparently now designated as a park, where begging and soliciting are prohibited. Then we continued down a crazily busy Central Avenue, where partygoers were out in force. I wondered why any adults, others than those wanting to cause trouble, would want to go down there. It was a loud and frightening atmosphere, and I wanted to escape from there as soon as possible.

We stopped at a park and gave a number of lunches to grateful people for whom the park would be home that night. One was hitching a ride to Missouri, where he said there was work. He'd eaten little all day and was grateful for the food and encouragement. As a couple of individuals passed by we quickly returned to the van. We knew them as drug dealers, well known in that area of town, with whom we had no wish to have an encounter.

Heading back to an earlier spot we noticed a few more people had gathered and the refrain was, "We're thirsty!" We gave out a variety of beverages and sack lunches and moved on. It was getting close to calling it a night.

While heading back to our parking lot we saw a young woman carrying a baby. I asked her if she was okay. She said she was. I had doubts, but there wasn't much I could do. I breathed a quick prayer for the two of them, and a couple of minutes later we arrived back at Joy Junction. It was eleven forty-five and seventy-seven degrees outside.

With the excitement of the evening's outreach over, my stomachache returned. Apparently, a stomach bug was making the rounds. *Oh well,* I thought as I cranked up the country music. *This, too, shall pass.*

Our Case Manager: A Day in the Life

The term "case manager" is heard a lot, but I wonder how many people know what exactly a case manager does. I asked Carl Valles, our case manager at Joy Junction, to tell me about a typical recent day—if there is such a thing.

He said he begins by reading all his e-mails. There was one that demanded prompt attention—a concern from an on-duty supervisor about a Joy Junction guest. The supervisor was worried about an elderly individual who was having difficulty walking and perhaps also suffering from some sort of dementia. Carl checked around the property to look for her but discovered she had already left Joy Junction for the day. He asked the supervisor to alert him as soon as she came back, assuming she might.

Back in his office, Carl started researching topics for the next Christ in Power (CIPP) life-recovery program class he was scheduled to teach. There were a number of options. Although money management and interviewing skills are a core part of the class curriculum, Carl said there are some other issues that are just as important. He opted for common courtesy and understanding of others and narrowed down what is quite a big topic to "Five Ways to Be Thoughtful and Considerate of Others." Having decided on this topic, Carl then went to all the Bible verses relevant to the topic and printed them out as resource materials for the upcoming class attendees. He spent about an hour going over the material.

Carl's intercom buzzed. It was a call from a supervisor asking if he was able to speak to a new guest about the programs we have available at Joy Junction. Carl said he would be happy to, but it would have to wait until he had completed an already scheduled appointment with a member of CIPP. During that meeting, Carl talked with the individual about his goals, what plans he had to reach them, and what resources he needed prior to his departure from Joy Junction at some point after program graduation.

Following that meeting, Carl then met with the new guest, a single woman questioning her faith due to ongoing tragedies. Carl learned she had been a nurse at one point in her life until her license was suspended. She gave up her parental rights to her daughter, lost everything, and ended up becoming homeless. Carl answered all her questions and assured her he has an open-door policy for his office and to come back if he could help her further.

Next, Carl met with a guy who was struggling with active addiction. Carl told him he needed to do whatever it took to get a grip on the issue.

Time for lunch. Carl said, "At lunch I went out and greeted residents who are familiar faces and those who are not. I discovered that people really enjoy it when someone greets or remembers them where there are so many faces in the crowd. I had my own lunch in my office a little later while continuing to work."

Carl next took a call from a case manager at the Los Lunas Correctional Facility. The individual wanted to know whether he could refer someone to us upon his release. After finding out the man's criminal history, Carl and Denis Billy, our resident services supervisor, determined he would not be an appropriate fit for Joy Junction.

Then Carl worked on schedules of volunteer hours for CIPP participants and another (less intensive) Joy Junction program, Hands Up (HUP). He analyzed the completed volunteer hours for program participants, reviewed job search logs and looked on our computer database for those who had not turned in their job searches.

Carl said he next looked around for program members who were on property but not complying with their program requirements. "I found one participant. We talked, and it turned out all he really wanted was a secure place to stay, that he was not interested in his spirituality or employment," Carl said. He added, "I told him he was no longer on the program, but case management is available to all residents at Joy Junction whether they are programmers or not. He thank me and JJ and stated he understood."

A woman for whom Carl did research concerning student loans came to his office excited that she might have the opportunity to return to school and get a job in a new profession. Carl said, "She was very happy with the news she received and felt hopeful."

The supervisor called again about a new guest couple needing help. They said they'd had bus tickets to Denver stolen and only wanted to stay at Joy Junction until they had the funds to get to Colorado, as they had money and support there. Carl gave day labor job information to them, and the guy told Carl he was already familiar with Labor Ready in Colorado, having worked with them before. They felt it wouldn't take a lot of time to get the funds needed for the tickets. They thanked Carl for the information.

A new guest needing encouragement was next on Carl's agenda. "When I asked her how I could be of assistance, she broke down crying, saying she was so lost. She had been off drugs for almost a month but felt that she needed help to remain clean and get her life back together." After hearing about our CIPP program, she decided to join. She completed the necessary application.

Carl said, "We talked some more, and I was able to provide words of encouragement and understanding." He added, "She hugged me and thanked me and JJ for letting stay here."

Next it was paperwork. Carl completed the background check for this new application and let Denis know.

Last thing for Carl to do was to complete his daily activity log for Jennifer Munsey, our chief operations officer. Now he could call it a day and go home. How does your day at work stack up compared to that?

Food for Thought

Is there anything you as an individual can do in your community to help lift families out of homelessness? Can you think of any prevention strategies to ward off homelessness before it starts? How can you encourage your community to improve its response to family homelessness?

Joy Junction provides well over 200,000 meals a year to homeless women, men, children, and families. This is a major accomplishment, but it is only a drop in the bucket, and much more remains to be done. If you want to help, there is no time like the present.

You can also make an effort on your own. For example, you can keep food kits in your car to give away to those on the streets. You can have some fast-food gift cards on hand for the same purpose. You can collect your recyclables (cans and bottles) and donate them to homeless people who collect them for money. You can donate to a food drive, or organize a program at your church to be a clearinghouse for food donations. What other ways can you think of to get involved in feeding the homeless?

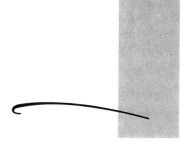

FORTY-EIGHT HOURS AT JOY JUNCTION

H ave you ever been curious what goes on behind the scenes at a large homeless shelter? Here is a look at a recent forty-eight hours (six shifts) at Joy Junction. It is perhaps a bit "routine," but a regular schedule, regular meals, and some assurance of normalcy are an essential part of recovery for many of our guests.

For the homeless, the only thing predictable in their lives before coming to Joy Junction is the unpredictability of where the next meal is coming from and where they will sleep that night. All that uncertainty and the danger of life on the streets results in a pretty predictable dose of depression. Sometimes, homeless people try dousing the horror of their circumstances with the inappropriate use of alcohol or illegal drugs.

Monday Afternoon

At 2:30 p.m. Sally, a resident services supervisor, was disappointed when she went to get hygiene supplies to hand out. "Out of five items we needed, we only had two: toothbrushes and tampons."

At 3:00 p.m. the Joy Junction van delivered a woman seeking refuge from a domestic violence situation. Sally signed her in, collected all the necessary information, and asked her if she would like to meet with our case manager. Sally began assessing available space for the evening at 3:10 p.m.

At 4:00 p.m. the domestic violence victim met with our case manager.

The multipurpose area was full of tired and hungry people at 4:50 p.m. The children were still full of energy, and conversation filled the room.

At 6:00 p.m. the multipurpose area was cleared of tables so we could begin sweeping and mopping the floors in preparation for the portable mattresses being laid out for the evening's sleep. Some guests seemed frantic to get their mats and kept asking Sally when they could have them.

Sally said the after-dinner sign-in process went very well on this day. "Most people were patient as we signed them in. Linen was distributed, and one by one they made their beds for the night. Some were asleep before the lights went out at 9:00 p.m."

Sally said, "The most challenging part of my shift today was making sure we were able to get everyone we could in under the roof for the night, especially when we were filling up to capacity. I wanted to be able to squeeze one more person in, to see relief in a face, to make sure everyone was safe."

Monday/Tuesday Graveyard Shift

At 10:00 p.m. resident services supervisor Sophie came on duty. As she prepared for her shift, she learned that a 911 call had been placed for an overnight guest who had been complaining of nausea and was having difficulty breathing. Sophie talked with her while waiting for the emergency vehicle, and everyone hoped whatever was going on with her was not serious.

The emergency medical personnel arrived at 10:10 p.m. After evaluating the woman they transported her to a hospital at 10:25. While the EMTs were still on property, another female overnight guest asked for emergency services. She told Sophie she smoked a cigarette that may have been laced with a drug. In any event, she felt drugged and sick. The EMTs evaluated the woman and took her by ambulance to the hospital as well.

At 12:30 a.m a guest told Sophie there was an alarm going off in one of our buildings. Sophie walked over to the barracks and found all the residents had been awakened and were standing in the hallway. "I knocked on the door to room six, where the alarm was going off, but no one answered. I went in and found no one in the room, but the alarm clock was blasting away. A check revealed the couple assigned to the room were not on property. Sophie told everyone it was okay to go back to their rooms.

The Albuquerque Police department brought in a single female needing a place to stay for the night at 1:30 a.m.

At 2:00 a.m. the two women who had earlier gone to the hospital arrived back at Joy Junction. They didn't have any medical discharge paperwork. When asked about it, they said they hadn't been seen by a doctor. They were told it would be several hours before they could be examined, and so they left. The rest of the night passed with no further incidents.

Just before 6:00 a.m. Sophie reflected on her shift. "There have been people of all ages here tonight. I often think that this must be the only place they can come to lay their heads. I suppose they know we are doing our best to keep everyone of them as safe as possible. All the residents seemed at peace as they slept. The most challenging thing on my shift was trying to resolve several issues at once, and trying to calm down the man whose wife had a medical issue (she was the one the EMTs transported to the hospital). I reassured him we would drive him to the hospital so he could be with her."

Tuesday

At 5:45 a.m. resident services supervisor John arrived at Joy Junction for his 6:00 a.m. to 2:00 p.m. shift, which began with a full house of overnight guests.

Six a.m. is "wake up" at Joy Junction. This is a little later than some other shelters, but why not? What is the point of getting our overnight guests up earlier to send them back into the streets where nothing is even open yet?

The wake-up this morning got off to a slow start, but John said it is like that occasionally. "Many of the overnight residents probably wanted a bit more sleep. Some of them came to the shelter quite late last night, and they were tired from being on the streets. No wonder they had difficulty getting to sleep."

Breakfast time at Joy Junction is 7:00 a.m. "It can seem chaotic getting everyone up, getting the mats put away, and serving breakfast," said John. "However, the overnight guests certainly appreciated the breakfast, which this morning was fried eggs and sausage. The coffee gave everybody a jump-start to their day, but the challenge continued because once breakfast was over we had to quickly get things cleaned up and ready for the Life Recovery Class."

At 8:30 a.m. the organization Health Care for the Homeless came on the Joy Junction campus for their regular visit.

At 9:00 a.m. it was time for our regular Christ in Power Life Recovery Program (CIPP) class. Once the class started, John had a few minutes to catch his breath. The Joy Junction resident services manager was the class teacher, and his topic that day was overcoming denial. During the CIPP class, John distributed weekly supplies to the dorms and barracks, while the maintenance crew continued working on painting the back hall and the women's restroom in the multipurpose building.

The class ended at 11:00 a.m., and shortly thereafter, the resident services manager met with CIPP volunteers to discuss any issues they may be experiencing. At the same time, a large volunteer group from Sandia Valley Church of the Nazarene came in for a tour of the facilities and to help serve lunch.

Meanwhile, in another part of our multipurpose building, veteran minister and former Joy Junction Chaplain Gene Shiplet was sharing God's love with our guests in his own unique way. His morning hours were spent answering residents' various personal questions and taking a hospital case worker's call regarding our facility and how we might be able to help her client.

At 2:20 p.m., Gene met with a resident and explained to him he needed to stay focused on his program and not let any of the single women pull him off course.

Gene was to have met for counseling with a couple having marital issues at 2:30 p.m. and was frustrated when they failed to show. He did meet Sally for a chat at 3:00 p.m., just to see how she was doing. At 3:20 p.m. Gene's manager came to him with a sensitive matter for which he asked his counsel. They discussed the situation and came to an agreed-upon conclusion.

A bit earlier, at 1:45 p.m., Sally had come on duty and it was time for John to turn the reins back over to her. Sally found she would be flying solo on the shift, as her co-worker had called in sick. She told herself, "You can do this alone, Sally. You have done it many times before." At 2:15 p.m., after bringing herself up to speed on what was going on at Joy Junction, Sally went to the supply area to get personal hygiene items for distribution to guests. "Today my trip was better than yesterday because we had more of the items needed. I never like coming back empty-handed."

At 2:40 p.m. Sally arranged for someone to cover for a few minutes for the program volunteer who was manning the guard shack. Then, a few minutes later, Chaplain Gene invited Sally into his office for a few minutes, wanting to know how things were going.

At 4:00 p.m. Sally did some computer updates on what spaces were still available at the facility. Having an accurate idea of accessible occupancy is an important component of the resident supervisor's job.

While Sally is on duty, she is constantly answering never-ending questions from our guests. Sometimes they are looking for personal hygiene items or articles of clothing (especially socks), asking about the van runs, looking for something to eat, or asking for prayer. Children ask for footballs and basketballs and other items for sports and games. You name it, someone is always asking for something.

At 4:45 p.m. the first van rolled in with a full load of hungry people. Today it was uncomfortably hot and the people looked beat. Even so, Sally said the kids had seemingly never-ending energy. At 5:00 p.m. it was time for dinner. A call was made for servers to help, and we were blessed with volunteers who worked before they themselves were served. Very few complained about the meal that was prepared, and the kitchen staff did a wonderful job, as they always do, of keeping everyone fed.

The multipurpose room transforms time and again into a dinner hall; after dinner, it becomes (as on every other day) a huge bedroom. This transformation takes about an hour. While the room is being cleared, swept, and mopped, people gather outside and converse, mostly talking about their day. Everything went well tonight.

At 7:30 p.m. it was time for overnight sign-ins. The process went smoothly with quick distribution of mats and linens.

The 9:00 p.m. lights out was at 9:30 tonight. There was no specific reason for this. Just a busy evening.

At 9:45 p.m. another day was almost done. Sally was very tired and ready to go home as her replacement came on site. "The best and most challenging part of my shift today, like yesterday, was making sure we were able to provide room for everyone who needed a roof over their heads. This is not always easy in these trying times, and it is not always even possible."

Tuesday/Wednesday Graveyard Shift

It was now time for Sophie to relieve Sally and begin her overnight shift. And at 12:30 a.m. the same alarm that went off the night before went off again! The couple occupying the room had still not yet returned. This time, Sophie disconnected the alarm from the electrical outlet. The evening continued without incident until a woman with a history of mental issues came to the office upset that someone off property had broken into her car. She said the previous owner still had a set of keys to her vehicle, and she suspected he might be the culprit. Sophie was able to calm and reassure the woman that things were going to be okay.

At 6:00 a.m. it was time for Sophie to get some well-earned rest when John came back on duty.

Wednesday

John oversaw another wake up at Joy Junction with the lights on at 6:00 a.m. followed by the rush to put the mats away and set up the tables for breakfast at 7:00—sausage and pancakes this morning.

At 8:00 John administered a urinalysis (UA) drug test to some guests. He said, "This is not always an easy thing to do, but it is necessary to ensure the safety and security of the residents at Joy Junction. Many of the residents here are fighting addictions to drugs or alcohol, so it's important to try keeping the environment drug free. The first couple I had to UA was not particularly happy about being asked to cooperate with the test—and for good reason! They tested positive for THC (marijuana). Because they were new and had used drugs prior to getting here, we gave them a chance to get clean. They would be retested in a few weeks. We can only hope our residents take advantage of the chances they are given."

It was now time for John and the CIPP program participants to get the multipurpose building cleaned up and the tables rearranged for the Life Recovery Class. They made sure the trash was taken out and the other numerous daily chores completed. Collecting and filing the intake paperwork from the new guests who came in last night was also on the agenda.

"During this time I was also approving a number of clothing vouchers to our thrift store down the block," added John. "Some of the overnight guests had nothing but the clothes they were wearing." John also fielded a multitude of questions from overnight guests, some of whom were staying at Joy Junction for the first time. Questions like,

"When is the next van going downtown?" and "When is the case manager in?" John let guests know the chaplain was on hand and available to counsel with them.

At 8:45 a.m. there was good news from the UA drug test results. John said, "A couple I had to test came up clean, which is always good to see. A small victory for that couple this morning."

The Life Recovery class begins at 9:00, so a few minutes before the start of the class, "I was calling for program participants to get signed in," John said. He made sure stragglers finished up their cigarettes and got inside. Today's topic? God's unconditional love.

At 10:15 a.m. John inventoried items in overnight storage and sent to them to the resident services manager. Between then and lunch, he cleaned out lockers and tended to routine guest needs.

Guests came on the JJ property for lunch at noon and picked up a couple of John's ditty bags from long-term storage.

At 12:30 p.m. there was more mopping and sweeping. "After lunch I helped a former program participant get his belongings from our storage by the laundry," John reported. "I also cleared out some lockers. Storage and lockers are very limited, so it's an ongoing battle to clear out abandoned lockers and remove abandoned bags to make room for current residents." Once that was completed, John worked on his shift report to pass on the significant events or shift information to his co-workers.

At 2:00 p.m. it was time for John to finish his shift and hand the baton on to the next supervisor.

Postscript

On the Friday just before this forty-eight hour period, one of our staff was asked to work with a seventy-eight year old man who needed help. She admitted, "I panicked! The shelter has seen many of Albuquerque's senior citizens come and go. When I encounter this population, I am immediately anxious, because, in all honesty, there is nowhere for them to go. Usually, Adult Protective Services (APS) can do very little to help them if there is no abuse or neglect, or if they are not being taken advantage of."

The man already had a caseworker with APS, so we contacted the caseworker who assured us that our mutual client "was of sound mind and body." The trouble was this was not a factual statement. The gentleman appeared to have a lot of memory problems, so our case manager spent the entire weekend trying to keep him safe and from leaving the property. She was exhausted by Monday when she came to work and discovered the man left Joy Junction just before she arrived. She said, "I was struck with a horrible realization that I was somehow going to be held responsible if something bad happened to him." She called APS to let them know what had happened and was told, "Don't worry. He does that all the time."

How could she not worry? Then she received a call on Monday from the emergency room at Presbyterian Hospital saying they had our resident and he was fine. The gentleman was returned to Joy Junction on Monday morning in good health and good spirits.

We were very pleased to find out that the man had an exit plan in place and would soon be receiving permanent housing. This is huge, because a lot of our residents never get to this point. We are blessed knowing he will be okay.

Food for Thought

Joy Junction is like other emergency shelters in that we can help only a fraction of the rapidly increasing homeless population. What can we do on a nationwide level to end homelessness? What could you do in your own community to offer emergency food, housing, and utility assistance to the homeless? What local ministries, services, or organizations can you connect with to help?

"Say My Name": The Homeless Are People, Not Statistics

We have had many unusual incidents at Joy Junction. On most evenings, sign-ins for the evening's overnight shelter go relatively smoothly. Our guests arrive, sign the log, and if they are new to Joy Junction, fill out an intake form. Then their name is called, and they receive their bed assignment and linens. It's really pretty simple.

On one evening, a male guest arrived and filled out the intake form. He was told to wait just a bit for his name to be called. Thirty minutes passed, and he became agitated. "How do I get my bed? How do I get my bed?" he asked, rapid-fire.

"We'll call your name, sir. Just give us a few more minutes and then you'll get your bed assignment and linens."

More time passed and the process repeated itself. "How do I get my bed? How do I get my bed?" We told him the process three different times. After the third time he said, "Say my name. Say it now!" We told him when everything was ready we would say his name and he would get his bed.

The scene repeated itself several more times. "Come outside your office and say my name." One of our resident service staff followed him outside and said his name. Then she told him, "When we have everything ready, I'll do it just like that."

"Say it again."

She said the man's name again and returned to her office.

A few minutes later, he was in another supervisor's office. "Say my name," he demanded.

She said his name, and the man received his bed assignment and linens for the evening.

Later, he returned to the first manager and said, "Say my name!" She obliged him, after which he spun around and left. The interesting thing was he did not even end up staying for the entire evening.

What distressed this man to this extent? Why was he so fixated on hearing his name? What gifts lie dormant in him? How will he survive in a world with no use for the mentally ill? We don't know. All we can do now is pray, saying his name before the Father.

Vagrants Are People, Too

A few years ago, there was a fire in a local and abandoned motel in Albuquerque. "Vagrants" were speculated to be the cause, according to a local official speaking on a newscast at the time of the fire.

Sometime after the fire, a Joy Junction staff member and I spent the afternoon doing outreach to some of the economically challenged and just plain desperate areas of our city. One of the locations we visited was an old abandoned motel where several people were living in rather squalid circumstances. They would probably be referred to as "vagrants."

I don't like that word; for years I have had a problem with it as it is very negative and impersonal. When we depersonalize people by calling them vagrants, many of us do so to relieve ourselves of any responsibility for those who have no place to live. According to the dictionary, a vagrant is "someone who has no established home and drifts from place to place without visible or lawful means of support." Traditionally a vagrant was thought to be one who was able to work for his maintenance, but preferred instead to live idly, often as a beggar. The punishment for this behavior (or lack of behavior) ranged from branding and whipping to conscription into the military services and transportation to penal colonies.

Historically in the United States, vagrancy is punishable when it is accompanied by the act of begging. But usually local authorities do not wish to arrest vagrants because this would involve the financial burden of supporting the offender. Instead, most communities just encourage vagrants to move along.

While the term *vagrant* is negative and impersonal, vagrants are not impersonal. They are real human beings just like you and me. They have names, parents, perhaps siblings. They have emotions, hurts, hopes, and fears, just as any of us. And just like all of us, they want to be loved. They were created by God in their mother's wombs with a body, a soul, and a spirit. Jesus Christ died for their sins. Despite how some vagrants look and even smell, we would do well to remember that, in his own day, Jesus himself would have been considered a vagrant. In a way, the business of salvation is the *vagrant transformation business*.

It is harder to dismiss someone when we describe them in terms like this, isn't it?

Returning to the old abandoned motel where we visited several people, what do you think was going through their minds as they spent the night there? Were they perhaps thinking about parents and children whom they hadn't seen for years? Or about failed opportunities and relationships? Or shattered hopes and dreams that led them to make a series of bad choices that may have included alcohol and drug abuse? Or were they just merely thinking how cold it was and what they could do to keep warm?

Who knows what circumstances resulted in these people breaking into this abandoned motel? Am I justifying that behavior? No, but I wonder whether some of us may have made similar choices if we had been faced with the misfortunes experienced by most of those we dismiss as "vagrants."

Rather than dismissing people who don't fit into our cozy, cultured perspective and consequently encouraging them to move on (and let's admit it, that is so much easier to do than to deal with the problem), isn't it time we addressed the issues leading to those behaviors and provided help in a spirit of compassion? With the Lord's help, that is what I have dedicated myself to do, and that is the intent of the emergency ministry behind Joy Junction.

I hate to think what would have happened to me if years ago people wrote me off as a worthless "vagrant." In February 1982, I arrived homeless and almost penniless in Santa Fe, New Mexico. I was miserable and felt like a complete failure. If the Great American Dream was still possible, it was a reality I was far from experiencing.

I had no friends I could call for help, but the next day after spending the few dollars I had on a motel room, I did go to a local church. There I was warmly greeted and given the opportunity to tell my story to a church member who offered me a place to stay in the government-assisted housing where he and his family were living. A few days later I was offered a place to stay in the basement office of a local businessman, who put me to work painting some of his apartments. After witnessing my attempts at house painting, he probably wondered about his judgment, but he was gracious enough to keep me around until I found steady work at a local hotel.

Here's the moral of the story. These individuals could have quite easily written me off as a vagrant or beggar who should be sent on his way. It would have been much easier for them to have done that. But instead, they assumed responsibility for me, prayed for my situation, and freely gave me the tools I needed to help me get back on my feet again.

Joy Junction's thirty years of operation are a direct result of the Lord's faithfulness but also of the efforts of God's people all along the way. Without their kindness, generosity, and interest in growing the Kingdom, I have no idea where I would be today.

So try it. If you are part of a church family, and vagrants, also known as homeless persons, come to you for help, try to help them. That may mean a smile and a meal or referring them to Joy Junction or a shelter in your area. Remember, your doing so will be in direct response to Deuteronomy 15:11, which says, "There will always be poor people in the land. Therefore I command you to be openhanded toward your fellow Israelites [your brothers and sisters] who are poor and needy in your land."

You never know what results it might produce.

Joy Junction: Where Hope Outshines Fear

Christ in Power life recovery-class participants were asked to list their top hopes and fears, and their answers underscore the importance of hope in all of our lives.

It turns out that fear comes in all sizes. There are the normal ones, such as fear of spiders, snakes, death, the future, heights, needles, and drowning. Other normal ones reared their heads, like the fear of losing a husband or wife, losing a child, the death of parents, relapse into an addiction, and losing one's faith in God. Not being around and not meeting life's goals is a major fear.

Several participants listed fear of abandonment, not being a good-enough mom or dad, rejection, loneliness, losing oneself, hurting a son or daughter, and being a failure. Other fears listed included being afraid of failure, of God, and of "turning into my mother." The fear of dying alone ranked high, and so did the fear of not going to heaven when Jesus comes back. Class members who battled addictions were afraid of backsliding, of having their hearts broken again, and of dying lonely and painful deaths.

Now go back and reread that last paragraph. Think about the profound nature of what some of our guests are saying. Think about those fears. Do you fear any of these things? Probably at least a few. Will you say a prayer for everyone who contributed to this list?

Our class instructor at the time asked, "What can possibly help alleviate such fears, especially when they are combined with homelessness?

Can hope outshine fear even in a homeless shelter?" His answer is, "I would say a resounding yes!"

Along with their top fears, class participants were asked to list their top hopes. Some of their hopes included "watching my children grow up strong and healthy." "Building a stronger and healthier relationship with God." "Being thankful, not judgmental, to the things God puts in front of me." "Having a successful and strong commitment to God and to die without regrets." "Having a loving, strong, and healthy relationship with another person." "Helping others grow and find the thing they need in their lives." "Finding love for myself."

One person wrote that his fondest hope was "reconciliation with my children, a home, honesty, peace, and a return to the Lord." Another hoped for "a house of my own, to be used by God, to finish college, open a recovery home, and to find happiness." Others had hopes of renewing wedding vows, growing old with their spouse, having a clear mind, and developing a heart that didn't break so easily.

A class member spoke of wanting the ability to "pray aloud in front of a crowd without crying, see my children without feeling shame for what I put them through, and the forgiveness of others."

Don't we all want a stronger and healthier relationship with God? Don't we all want to die without regrets? Don't we all want most of the things our CIPP group hopes for? How do we get there? How did these precious homeless souls get on the right path, the path of hope?

The class instructor said he thought he knew. "I believe they began to see, through their life recovery classes, that their Creator is much more than 'the man upstairs.' He is a loving God who pursues a relationship with them, even to the point of sacrificing his only Son. He values them as beings he made in his divine image. This, coupled with a supportive community, makes hope shine brighter than their fears."

Food for Thought

I believe the Lord brings each person to Joy Junction for a reason. For some people, it is to help them survive in a world that is beyond their handling. For others, it is to give them a certainty to their future. For many, it is to give them an opportunity to grow as men and women and to develop a close relationship with the Lord. Do you believe everyone's life has been worked out according to God's plan? If not, what do you do with a verse like Ephesians 1:11? "In him we were also chosen, having been predestined according to the plan of him who works out everything in conformity with the purpose of his will."

Most of us don't want to consider what we would like written on our tombstone, but it's a good question, nevertheless. What would you like to see written on yours?

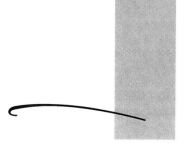

"THOSE PEOPLE DON'T WANT HELP!" OR DO THEY?

After thirty-four years of helping New Mexico's homeless, I am convinced that there is nobody who doesn't "want" help.

While an addict's negative response to what would seem like sensible assistance—a trip to a detox or homeless shelter—may result in the statement, "Well, he doesn't want help," we need to go beyond that.

People don't set out to be addicts. Someone's slide into addiction often begins with an abuse of alcohol or drugs to mask unbearable emotional pain. The substance soon becomes a cruel taskmaster, and the quicksand of addiction begins. A bed in an apartment is exchanged for a precarious existence on city streets, where an addict wanders and wobbles from one fix or high to the next.

There is an emotional and physical component of successful recovery. While we hope addicts will take the first step when we want them to, that doesn't always happen. Until addicts are willing and able to walk down recovery road, their lives can often negatively impact many other people who cross their paths.

A drunk person's lack of inhibitions often results in using the bathroom in public and sleeping—after drinking a few cans of beer—outside someone's business. That and similar behavior results in consequences such as anti-homeless spikes being placed in areas frequented by the homeless and dividers being placed on public benches to stop the homeless from sleeping there.

My recent Facebook posting of an *Upworthy* article dealing with an attempt to make these anti-homeless spikes a bit more comfy had a local businessperson a little upset. Acknowledging that it's a difficult problem for which she didn't have a ready answer, she asked, "What about the destruction and trashing of private property by those who refuse help?" She explained she used to manage a small shopping center where homeless people would sleep in the bushes. Every Monday, her crew would fill a thirty-three-gallon trash can full of beer cans and bottles they found in the areas where the homeless had spent their night.

She added, "We had to hose off the doorways in the courtyard in the mornings because they would urinate on the doorsteps and defecate in the parking lot. They would vomit on the walls." Talking with these individuals didn't work, she said. They were either too drunk or too combative. An offer of a ride to a shelter wasn't welcome, either.

"We finally took the bushes out," she said. "They would sleep in the courtyard. We would have to call the police because of the safety and cleanliness we owed the customers of our tenants. What is the answer? Some simply don't want help."

Barbara has a point, so I posed this question on Facebook. "What is the answer for those who are addicts and for whatever reason are unable to receive or decline help? As a community, how do we help those in the throes of addictive behavior while helping and preserving the rights of someone like Barbara?"

Samantha said we aren't commanded to love just those who want to be loved, or help only those who want to be helped. She continued, "Even people 'who don't want to be helped' are people, and they have hearts that were terribly broken somewhere along the way." However, she conceded, "If your property were being violated to such an extent, some type of legal protection would probably be necessary."

Samantha encouraged everyone to keep praying rather than give up or write people off. "We forget the power of prayer. We can do all we can do in the flesh, and sometimes it is simply a heart issue. Keep praying for these people; you might be the only one doing it."

Pam, another Facebook friend, was clear about how she felt. She said those people who feel business owners or city officials are hard-hearted for wanting to remove the homeless from certain areas should "be the ones to go from place to place and clean up the trash, urine, poop, needles."

She continued, "They would be the ones picking up the tab for the trash bags and other materials needed to clean the places . . . They would be working with zero pay as well. These are all things the shop owners have to do. I think their tune would change real quick when they saw the 'dirty' side of it all."

So what is the answer? One way to start working toward a solution is to talk to people who have "been there." I asked our resident services manager at Joy Junction to talk with some of our guests who at one point had been through the grips of alcohol/drug addiction to explain what it had done to them.

A fifty-six-year-old woman who said she had been "drinking, drugging, and having sex" since she was thirteen said the short answer is what her addiction "didn't" do to her. She listed, "The unremembered days, blackouts, drunken sex, STDs, the violence, hurt to family and friends, the hurt to my self-esteem, resentment of myself, my broken bones, being beaten and suicidal thoughts."

She recalled sleeping in a pup tent by the Sacramento River under a bridge and bushes. "I was hungry, thirsty and scared. Many times I've been used and abused and with all of this comes defecating, urinating in public, and soiling myself." However, good news came. "After many years of trying to quit, I did it by just trying and realizing that my addiction was getting me nowhere. It worked, but I'm still working on myself here at JJ."

Another of our guests was formerly addicted to heroin and meth. She said her addiction has caused her multiple problems, including loss of her children to her parents. She said, "I still feel so much guilt for not getting myself together before it was too late. This caused me to have a very bad relationship with my family. It has also caused many physical problems, such as permanent track mark scars, Hep C, and messed up teeth. My addiction is the reason for my homelessness."

While using, this woman said she would crash at a friend's house and also in doorways. The situation got so bad that earlier this year she ended up in hospital as the result of an infection incurred by shooting up in her leg. While in the hospital she decided to get clean. "I did not want to end up dead like my friend who overdosed on heroin. After I got out of the hospital, I got on Suboxone and came to JJ. I've been clean for almost seven months."

Almost as an afterthought she added, "By the way, I've never defecated on myself, but I've urinated in public and on myself. It was gross. Actually, my pants were soaked when I got to JJ."

A male guest told us, "My defects really made a mess of my life." He said that alcohol abuse and marijuana resulted in his getting fired from a job. Meth came later. He said that addiction made him think he was invincible.

He poignantly continued, "I remember one time when I was high. I was very well dressed, but there was no restroom around. I even looked for a bush, but found nothing. I had no choice but defecate in my pants. This caused me to get off of crack for a short time."

The businesswoman whose comment initiated the writing of this chapter said she knows this is a difficult situation for everyone concerned. She added, "My personal experience has been that some want and will accept help but there's a subset that don't. [It's a] hard place for those who care for the less fortunate, but also deserve to not have the things they've worked hard for destroyed. I don't know the answer."

So what was the turning point for the man who defecated in his pants? He said, "I remember that after I bagged the pants and threw them in a waste bin, my apartment manager found them and had them cleaned for me. What a great man! I'll never forget his generosity. That kind of kindness caused me to change my life and try to find help."

Food for Thought

Maybe kindness such as that manager's is a place at which a conversation could start. But the dialogue will need to be one embraced by the entire community. What do you think?

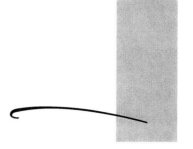

THIS IS OUR LIFE— JEREMY AND ELMA IN MINISTRY

Working at Joy Junction is a way of life more than a job.

It takes a calling and a commitment. While there's no such thing as a typical day for us, here are some highlights from a few recent ones.

First order of business upon waking up (like every day) was to check my BlackBerry to see if anything had happened overnight that needed immediate attention.

Of course, that occurred after a couple of middle-of-the-night checks of the Joy Junction security camera feed to my office at home. Even a late night/early morning trip to the bathroom in the middle of the night always ends up with a visit to my home office where I stay for a few minutes to see if everything looks okay. While we have staff on duty 24/7, an extra pair of eyes looking at the camera feed for a little while can always be a help. Running a mission providing food, shelter, and encouragement for the homeless means always being prepared for the unexpected and unusual and being grateful when it doesn't happen.

After a working lunch, we headed over to the Calvary of Albuquerque Campus, home of KNKT Radio, where I did a short, live on-air interview with Joy Junction friend and long-time radio host, Peter Benson. We have worked collaboratively with our friends at KNKT for many years. The ability to present a short, regular update about news at Joy Junction throughout the year (even when it is nowhere near the season of giving) has been a great blessing.

Following that, it was time to head over to 1037-The Oasis (a locally-owned jazz station), where we voice-tracked our regular Sunday morning show, which airs between 8 a.m. and midday. Owners Don Davis and Martha Whitman have been very gracious to us. This is another time where being on the air weekly gives us opportunity to share with the community what is going on with homelessness in general in Albuquerque and at Joy Junction in particular.

Next we headed to a restaurant close to the station for some networking. It's important to always keep the need out there before the public. I am a firm believer in the old adage, "Out of sight, out of mind." This event was put on by the Hispano Chamber of Commerce and 770-KKOB Radio. We stayed just over an hour and made some new friends as well as renewing acquaintances with old ones at KKOB.

We usually finish our workdays off with a visit to the shelter. After all, that's the reason why we spend countless hours every day crisscrossing the streets of Albuquerque, going from one meeting to another.

Then it was time for a quick visit to the grocery store before heading home at about 8 p.m. Elma took care of some household chores while I did a little exercise on my recumbent bike, got up to speed with the latest news on CNN, and made sure I was caught up with all the Joy Junction social-media updates for the day. We watched a little TV, prayed, and turned in.

Friday came quickly. The initial routine was very similar to Thursday, except we started the workday off with a visit to our corporate office in downtown Albuquerque where I spent some time with Joe Krall, our chief financial officer. In addition to signing checks, we also talked fund-raising strategy for the remainder of the year. Like most—maybe all—other missions, almost half of our budget is gathered in November and December. About 10 percent had been coming in during the last week of the year, so we had to tailor our strategy accordingly.

Following that we ate, firmed up some upcoming appointments, and then dropped by Bibles Plus to order some Life Recovery Bibles, the core of our Christ in Power life-recovery program at Joy Junction. We finished off the day meeting with a wonderful woman who is setting up an innovative new program, arranging meals and informal meetings between the homeless and interested members of the community.

Once home, the pace was much more relaxed, but the work was still there. I tried not to do too much as I wasn't feeling well. I ended off the day with Nyquil and slept relatively well.

Saturday was a late start but one which, while at a different pace, was still quite busy. While Elma cooked a delicious meal, I used the time to research and put together a message for the Saturday evening church service at Joy Junction. That always involves a skit based on a country song, followed by me giving a short teaching, with Elma concluding the service.

The most recent service focused on broken dreams, missed opportunities, and the importance of faith in Jesus. Our guests seemed to enjoy the experience.

On Sundays, Elma and I usually attend Calvary at Nob Hill, but this Sunday was a departure from that schedule. The annual event, Pennies for the Homeless High Tea and Fashion Show was taking place, and Joy Junction was one of a number of community organizations receiving funds from the event. This, of course, all occurred after the usual morning schedule I've described above. I also managed to get a bit of writing in before leaving while at the same time listening to one of my favorite shows, CNN's *Reliable Sources*.

We arrived at Hotel Albuquerque at about 11:30 a.m., just a few minutes early for what was a sold-out event. The emcee was former long-time KOB-TV anchor, Carla Aragon. What a delight to reconnect briefly with her and introduce her to Elma. We met a couple of delightful folk at lunch, a husband and wife who are a public defender and social worker respectively. I hope we'll see them down the road at Joy Junction.

After leaving Pennies for the Homeless, Elma and I made our way to an area department store for some shopping. Even then I wasn't really off duty, as I heard the familiar refrain, "Oh, you're Jeremy Reynalds from Joy Junction."

As I said, working for Joy Junction is a way of life more than a job. I'm so thankful to have found a life partner to share the journey with. Your prayers for us are so appreciated.

A DIVINE
APPOINTMENT

Since Elma has come into my life, we have sometimes acted as partners in ministry in the midst of situations we would not have expected. The following is an account of one of them.

It had been a good day, but a long one. I looked forward to a tranquil evening with my wife, Elma.

However, a slight detour was about to unfold. A need to visit a downtown ATM took us on a slightly different route to the shelter than the one we usually follow. We both believe it was the beginning of a divine appointment.

Driving along, I was attracted to a small, well-manicured lawn outside a church. I'd passed it several times before, but this time was different. On the lawn lay a woman dressed in a hospital gown (as well as other clothes). A few feet from her was a pineapple and a couple of backpacks. I have to admit that initially I really didn't want to stop. I was tempted to call the non-emergency line for the police so they could check on her. However, the police are busy and we were right there.

It was a "calling," I believe, that ultimately compelled us to check on the woman. I grabbed a fast-food gift card and walked slowly over to the woman, making sure I stayed a few feet away from her in case she was sleeping and would be scared if I woke her. However, she was awake. I told her who I was and gave her the card. She accepted it appreciatively.

She told me a little bit of her story. She said she had recently been released from an area hospital and had cracked ribs. While talking, she was writhing in pain.

The woman added that her friend had just walked a few hundred yards to a mission close by to see if he could get a blanket. She was unable to get pain medication due to not having any identification.

By this time, Elma had gotten out of the car and joined me on the grass. Wanting to relax her feet a little, Elma had taken off her shoes. Stepping on the grass, she said it was cold, I think more so than she expected. Lying there would definitely have been rather uncomfortable.

We asked the woman if she had heard of Joy Junction. She said she had, so I asked her if she would like a place to stay for the night. She said she would, so we called the office for a van to come and pick her up. While waiting for the driver, the woman's friend came back (without a blanket). He agreed to go with her to Joy Junction so he could watch over her for the night and call 911 to see if medical attention was needed.

Our driver came and took the two of them to Joy Junction. While I approved a longer stay, they only stayed the night and checked out the next morning.

I can't report any life-changing encounters from this story, and don't know the current whereabouts of this woman or her friend. I can tell you this was an opportunity for us to bring a kind word, a meal, and a safe place to stay for a woman in obvious distress. Need is all around us, so much so it can sometimes seem overwhelming. But if you keep your eyes open, God will use you to make a difference in people's lives in a way that you never thought possible.

Food for Thought

Be on the lookout. It may be your day for a divine appointment.

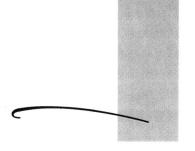

You Can Never Get Taken Advantage of When You Give with the Right Attitude

While I don't hesitate to give a fast-food gift card to someone in need, I rarely give cash. There are just too many ways it can be misused.

However, on the rare occasions I do give money, I only do so when I feel an inner prompting, which, as a Christian, I believe is from God. That way, I can never get "taken," because it is God's responsibility what happens to the money with which he entrusts me.

The afternoon of July 4 was one of those rare occasions. After checking in at Joy Junction to see how everything was going for our special Independence Day meal, my wife Elma and I went to do a little shopping.

It had been a good day. Everything was going well at the shelter and I was looking forward to some time enjoying watching Elma shop. Just as real men can eat quiche, they can also carve some time out to go shopping with their wives. If you want to know what makes your wife tick, go shopping with her and don't complain about how long she's taking! Okay, I have to admit that while Elma was trying on clothes, I was multi-tasking and working on my BlackBerry.

But back to my "rare occasion." I parked the car, and Elma and I were just preparing to walk across the parking lot to the store when a car stopped in front of us. The window was down, and a lady said, "Excuse me, but can you help me?"

She paused for a moment before continuing. "I'm from Silver . . ." She paused again, as if she wasn't quite sure whether that was where she was from. When I added the word, "City," she agreed and continued.

"I was just in a Circle K, put my bag down and it was taken. Could you help me with a tank of gas?"

When I asked how much that was, she said, "Twenty-six dollars."

Maybe it was a look of disbelief on my face at the high amount requested, or incredulity, because she pointed to a collapsible wheelchair in the back of her car and said, "I'm disabled, you know."

At that point it wasn't guilt, but an inner prompting that caused me to turn to Elma and ask her if we had any cash. We rarely carry money. She said we had a five-dollar bill. I told the woman we would help with five dollars cash, and asked if she was hungry. She said she was, so I also gave her a five-dollar gift card for a fast food chain.

She seemed very appreciative. I gave her a card for Joy Junction, and said if she didn't make it back to Silver City that she could call us and we would be happy to accommodate her.

Just before leaving, I told the woman, "Now, be sure to only spend the money for gas."

"I will," she assured us and drove off.

Elma and I continued our short walk across the parking lot and came to the door of the store. A tall man with a badge that identified him as the store manager asked us, "Did she ask you for money?"

I said she did, and that we gave her cash, a fast-food card, and my business card for Joy Junction.

He said, "Hmm. She's here every weekend doing that."

I also gave him my card, and told him to call Joy Junction for help with people he didn't want in his parking lot. He thanked me, and we continued on into the store.

236

A few minutes later, Elma and I talked and reflected on the incident. Yes, it seems obvious her story wasn't true, but what's also just as clear is she had a need. Otherwise why tell a story like that?

It reminded me of an incident in 2015 when we were both on the grounds of the Southern Philippine Medical Center in Davao. A woman with a sickly-looking child asked us for money, saying that her husband and one of her children had perished in a recent typhoon.

She said the hospital's emergency room was closed, and she was unable to get the care she needed for her baby.

We walked with her to the hospital ER, which was open, and helped her get signed in. Basically, her story didn't add up and a hospital employee was pretty insistent that her story was a scam. We still felt prompted to give her the equivalent of a couple of dollars and left.

Was the story a scam? Quite possibly, just like our experience here in Albuquerque. One way of looking at it would be to say it was a lie told out of need.

Were we "taken advantage of?" While some of you might believe we were, we would agreeably disagree. The few resources we gave on both occasions were given as unto the Lord, and we pray that on both occasions he will use them for his glory.

So maybe the lesson from both these incidents is to be discerning, but never become cynical. And remember, God loves a cheerful giver.

DO EVANGELICALS PRACTICE COMPASSION?

Bible Thumping the Homeless

It was just a simple update on Facebook, similar to one I have done many times before.

A generic picture of a couple of men sprawled out on the sidewalk, obviously experiencing hard times. My caption read, "If you see someone in need of shelter, let us know by calling Joy Junction at 800-924-0569. We'll do our best to help."

One response, posted on my personal Facebook page, astounded me. It was from a man who, according to his profile doesn't even live in Albuquerque, and as far as I know has never met me. It read, "Will you support men who refuse to work for a living, or insist on getting drunk or high all the time?"

The individual then went on to quote 2 Thessalonians 3:6–15 from the Bible. However, the way he did so was with the drumbeat of judgment and condemnation, not with the sound of love.

The passage is addressed to Christians who are busybodies, not working, and sticking their noses in other people's business. Verse 10 says, "If any would not work, neither should he eat." The verse was not referring to people who are in the grip of substance addiction.

I responded. "From an exegetical standpoint, the verses which you use refer to Christian brothers, and not those who haven't made a commitment to Christ. I added, "While neither alcohol or illegal drugs are allowed at Joy Junction, they are not the issue. For those who struggle with such issues, we look to what . . . issues have forced people to take refuge in them. Often it is a result of abuse or circumstances too awful for us to imagine. If we don't provide at least minimal assistance (in the hope that they will ultimately accept Jesus), how should we respond? Is it biblical to let people starve/go hungry on the streets? We believe not."

I haven't heard from him since.

Wanting to get an idea of what others thought of this man's response, I asked our Joy Junction Facebook fans for their input. They were quick to respond.

Enola said it's "amazing" how some people interpret the Scriptures. "Jesus came for the broken, the sick and those who had the ears to hear His message of love and forgiveness. These folks are broken, and a hand to lift up is a good and right thing to do. An introduction to Jesus and the Gospel along with a hot meal and a bed is a ministry from God."

I loved what Robin wrote. "It's odd to me that anyone could see a brother or sister in need and have to consult the Holy Bible regarding the recipient's worthiness of assistance. That just strikes me as odd, being it's only a few weeks past Christmas."

Robin added (tongue in cheek), "I guess it's nice that the Bible hadn't been written yet for the stable owner to read, and determine maybe Mary and Joseph were too pathetic to be pregnant and wandering around with no place to stay."

Richard said he sees homeless people near downtown every morning. "I make them coffee and give a few bucks and blankets. In the summer they just ask, 'Can I please use your water hose to shower and drink?' I cry a lot."

Thanks, Richard.

Linda said if we were in the position of those people shown in the picture, we for sure would want someone to help us out. She added if anyone is concerned about where exactly their money will go, then give support to area agencies, or buy the needy people you see a cup of hot coffee and a sandwich, or give a blanket. "I bet that deep down inside, you feel good about what you have done. It's very cold outside. We need to love and care more for our brothers and sisters out there."

Ron was also on target, commenting, "There will always be haters trying to discourage a helping hand. Wait a minute. Wasn't it Jesus who surrounded himself with people just like these?"

Yes, it was. John 8:7 reads that Jesus said, "Let any one of you who is without sin be the first to throw a stone at her."

Good words. If you're going to use the Bible to support your position, make sure what you're saying is what the Bible as a whole advocates. And in all things, make sure your motivation is one of love.

Joy Junction is firmly based on the Bible. However, we just don't feel comfortable condemning people. They feel bad enough already. We're content to be instruments of God's love, and let that bring them to wholeness.

Building Relationships by Meeting Needs

We shelter as many as three hundred people nightly and distribute 16,000 thousand meals plus a month. About 6,000 of those meals are served on our mobile feeding unit, the Lifeline of Hope, which crisscrosses Albuquerque seven days a week. In addition to the Lifeline meals being potential lifesavers, we also regard this street outreach as an integral part of relationship building.

Many of the people we assist have been hurt both emotionally and physically in unimaginable ways. For example, very recently we offered a man a hygiene kit, which he initially refused. Why? He said, "I get plenty from the trash." But he accepted the kit when I told him he deserved better than that. What had he experienced for him to think he deserved to retrieve things from the garbage like that?

We also gave three pairs of socks to a woman who was outside with bare feet. (We didn't have any shoes with us, or else we would have provided them.) She appeared intoxicated and quite possibly high. While some would disapprove, I believe Jesus approves of what we did.

Those are just two of the people we have come across recently in our Joy Junction work. It took years for these individuals to get to where they are, and it may take as long for them to get back on their feet. What are they going to do in the meantime? Who is going to care for them? We believe giving hungry and needy people a meal and more is the right thing to do—the Christian thing to do. Sadly, some evangelicals feel continuing to feed the hungry is "enabling" them. Really? I have yet to hear substantive solutions about what to do with all those people we should quit feeding. I guess the government could do it, but then how loudly would the conservatives be complaining?

Then there is the matter of a controversial tactic called "harm reduction." That's the giving of clean needles to drug addicts and condoms to sex workers and others. Like many evangelicals, I used to criticize harm-reduction workers as promoting irresponsible sex and illegal drug use. The problem was I had never bothered to talk with them. Once I did, I found they are not promoting random sex or drug use. What they are doing is trying to keep hurting people alive until they are ready to seek the recovery they need to stay alive. Shouldn't evangelicals be applauding that? I have said this earlier, and I will say it again: How can you preach the gospel to someone unless you keep him or her alive?

From my perspective as CEO of a large emergency homeless shelter ministry, something isn't smelling so sweet in evangelical paradise. I believe it is unconscionable not to feed a hungry person, or help a sick, addicted, hurting person trying to stay alive. What's wrong with evangelicals? Shouldn't we who say we have been forgiven so much by such a loving God want to share that same love with those in need?

The whole charged political atmosphere, with the religious right and religious left, just about drives me to despair. There are evangelical Christians who actually believe that the body politic is the most important determinant of our country's direction. They believe a change in this president or that congress is going to spell the success or failure of the nation. It seems to me evangelicals are being co-opted by a political party and reduced to a voting bloc. How tragic! Where is God in the picture? Is he in control or not?

There is only one way our country can be changed. If Christians will live out God's Word and quit judging or focusing on two or three "litmus-test" issues, the world will see we are Christians by our love. When that happens, profoundly amazing things will come to pass.

Food for Thought

What kind of a "Christian" are you?

What do you think is the most essential characteristic of a Christian?

TEACHABLE MOMENTS

To encourage communication, discussion, and involvement from a biblical perspective on the plight of homelessness in general, and Joy Junction in particular, let me offer some facts on homelessness in both Albuquerque and America.

Albuquerque Homeless Rate Drops—or Not?

The answer depends on whom you ask. Almost a year after the city of Albuquerque did its 2015 homelessness study, local media say the results show a downward shift in the homeless rate.

But, not so fast! All this positivity is based on something called the Point in Time (PIT) Count. Overseen by the Department of Housing and Urban Development (HUD), PIT is a count of sheltered and unsheltered homeless persons on a single night in January (www. hudexchange.info/hdx/guides/pit-hic/).

In January 2014, HUD counted 578,424 people on the streets and in shelters in the U.S., down 11 percent from 2007. The Department of Education, or DOE, which uses a different, more expansive methodology, reported that child and family homelessness doubled over the last decade.

"We get concerned when people start reporting that homelessness is way down, when we don't think that's accurate. So I think the numbers take on an importance beyond what's really justified," said Jeremy Rosen, director of advocacy at the National Law Center on Homelessness & Poverty.

The same story by Al Jazeera America reported that advocates say HUD's limitations start with how it defines homelessness. While the agency has a few programs that help those at risk of homelessness, the majority require that individuals fall into specific categories, namely living on the street, in temporary shelter, or those about to be evicted.

There may be hope on the horizon. The Homeless Children and Youth Act, or HCYA, has been introduced in both houses of Congress. Backers say it would force HUD to align its definition with those used by federal programs for low-income families and vulnerable minors, and reduce the requirements for proving homelessness. However, it has only a small chance of being enacted.

Interestingly, the National Alliance to End Homelessness (NAEH) is opposed to the bill, saying in a blog post, "There are no new resources attached to the bill, and the nation is already short a couple hundred million to effectively serve existing unsheltered families and unaccompanied children and youth."

So if I understand this correctly, the NAEH wants to keep the current and totally inadequate definition of homelessness, because while changing it would "increase" the number of homeless, there would be no more resources available to assist all of those newly "discovered" homeless individuals.

That is the most ridiculous thing I have ever heard. A change would allow us to have a better understanding of how many homeless people there really are, and it would strip away those glowing government pronouncements about how well we are doing in the fight to "end" homelessness. Having gotten a real understanding of the real situation, couldn't we then marshal resources to better meet the need?

I was intrigued that leaders in homeless advocacy said it will take more state and federal money to continue the work. Nothing was said about the private sector. That omission is curious. Nongovernmental support for the homeless is huge. Joy Junction, for example, receives no government funds. And while it's hard to estimate the dollar amount spent by private charities (admittedly some with government help) on the homeless, it's a vast amount and a lot of help. To name just a few, there are Catholic Charities, the 300 members of the Association of Gospel Rescue Missions, and the Salvation Army, which operates 7,546 centers in communities across the United States.

Since our Joy Junction staff works daily with our many homeless guests, I wondered what they thought about the much-vaunted "drop" in homelessness.

Carl Valles, Joy Junction case manager, was quite clear how he felt, when he said, "To state that homelessness is on the decease would be one of the most selfish statements I have yet to hear. One only has to look at the longer lines for public assistance agencies . . . and homeless camps springing up throughout America in lieu of shelters, and increased enrollment of homeless children in schools.

Joy Junction's Denis Billy said from his experience both here and working with the homeless in other states, that rather than being on the decrease, homelessness is on the increase.

Carol Nordhagen, our resident services supervisor, said all the talk about the number of homeless decreasing is due in part to "politically motivated objectives." She said when news consumers (who are often voters) see reports of lower homeless numbers, then they'll quite possibly think the party in power is really working on solving homelessness. And news reports, Nordhagen said, are quite often taken at face value. "John Q Public only has time to haphazardly listen to news reports, and is far too busy with his own survival in today's economy. He rarely gives [the accuracy of] news reports a second thought."

Nordhagen's sentiment is true, but let's remember this isn't usually a reporter's fault. Our local media reporters are mostly generalists, often having to turn out two or more stories in a single broadcast day shift.

For the most part, they don't have the time to question the accuracy or truth of a seemingly noncontroversial report (especially from HUD) that says homeless numbers are on the downswing. They may not even be aware of the debate raging nationally about the validity of HUD's PIT count.

So when you see that statistics show the rate of homelessness is decreasing, take a look at who's telling the story. The real picture is far from being as positive as some people—for whatever reason—would like you to think.

So Who Are the Homeless in America?

According to the latest government data, more than 600,000 Americans are homeless on a given night. Nearly a quarter of these are children, and a third live in unsheltered places like parks, cars, or abandoned buildings. The number of people who have been continuously homeless for more than one year, or experienced at least four episodes of homelessness over the last three years, is over 100,000, and two-thirds go unsheltered. There are more than 57,000 homeless veterans.

Statistics show that seventy-eight percent of all sheltered homeless persons are adults. Sixty-one percent are male. Sixty-two percent are members of a minority group. Thirty-eight percent are thirty-one to fifty years old. Sixty-four percent are in single-person households. Thirty-eight percent have a disability. Two-thirds have stayed in an emergency shelter or transitional housing program, and one-third have lived on the street or in an abandoned building or other place not appropriate for human habitation (streets, parks, alleys, subway tunnels, all-night movie theaters, roofs, stairwells, caves, campgrounds, and vehicles).

Violence against those without shelter continues to rise. It is very dangerous to be homeless. News stories of homeless people being killed for no reason are not uncommon in cities across America.

After you have read about some of our residents, I hope you have come to agree that there are hundreds of reasons why people are homeless. A lack of affordable housing, the limited scale of housing assistance programs, and an epidemic of home foreclosures have contributed to a booming housing crisis and to homelessness. The Department of Veterans Affairs recently released statistics showing that homelessness among Iraq and Afghanistan war veterans is sharply rising, despite new efforts to help them.

Another reason for the rise of homelessness is poverty, which is brought on, among other things, by the lack of employment opportunities and a decline in public assistance. The official poverty rate was fifteen percent in 2011, with 46.2 million people living in poverty. Homelessness and poverty are closely linked, because poor people cannot pay for housing (which absorbs most of one's income), food, childcare, health care, and education. With very limited resources, it is often housing that is dropped. Harvard's Joint Center for Housing Studies has shown that low-income households suffer an unprecedented housing cost burden, forcing many to choose between rent and food. Too often, homelessness is the result.

Other things contribute to homelessness, such as deficiency of available health care. A serious illness or disability can start a downward spiral to eviction and eventual homelessness. Many people are a mere paycheck or illness away from homelessness.

Domestic violence forces many women to choose between living in an abusive relationship or living in poverty and homelessness. Fifty percent of the cities surveyed in 2005 by the U.S. Conference of Mayors identified domestic violence as a primary cause of homelessness.

Mental illness is another cause of homelessness. According to a 2005 survey of the U.S. Conference of Mayors, approximately sixteen percent of the single adult homeless population suffers from some form of severe and persistent mental illness.

Alcohol and drug addiction also causes homelessness. Of course, not all who are addicted become homeless, but poor people who are addicted are clearly at increased risk of homelessness.

Whatever the reasons for it, there is a deep crisis of homelessness in our nation that must be ended. Ending it requires closing the gap between the need for housing and its availability. If our society recognizes housing as a basic human right, as it should, we must have policies that make sure it is available to all.

A society should not be measured by how much it does for the its wealthiest citizens, but rather what it does for its most vulnerable citizens. Too many in America would rather blame the homeless for their plight instead of trying to help them. The United States is the richest country on the planet, and we must do more to help those who need shelter and other emergency care.

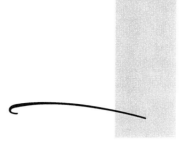

WHAT'S AHEAD FOR JOY JUNCTION?

The Bible says, "Where there is no vision, the people perish: but he that keepeth the law, happy is he" (Prov. 29:18 KJV). Close to thirty years after founding Joy Junction, my vision remains the same—and now I have Elma to share it with me.

We are two individuals, but we are one in vision: to provide food, shelter, recovery tools, and the love and encouragement of Jesus Christ to homeless, hungry, and distraught families. But the vision is so much bigger than it was at the beginning. Over the last two-and-a-half decades, the need for this ministry has grown exponentially as we have gotten busier than I could have ever imagined.

What are we thinking for the months and years ahead? I'm glad you asked.

Looking back, it seems just a short time ago that I came up the driveway of our fifty-two-acre property wanting to reach out to homeless families with food, shelter and the love of Jesus Christ.

We're currently sheltering as many as three hundred people nightly, and as I said earlier, providing more than 16,000 meals each month from a fully-licensed kitchen. With your prayers and support, we'll keep housing, feeding and encouraging homeless and hungry people.

But what lies ahead for us as a ministry? The future for Joy Junction is looking bright, with numerous renovations occurring at our aging property.

For the comfort of our guests we have upgraded the air conditioning at our main building, replaced windows, and put in a new driveway to help make visiting our facility a much less "bumpy" experience.

We're also working on installing a modest apartment complex as the Lord provides the resources. There are current details available at www.joyjunction.org.

Have you heard some of the government rhetoric about "ending" homelessness in the near future? Homeless people we have talked to, and more reasonable homeless advocates, don't think that's really likely. So, while I believe we will never "end" homelessness the way the term is bandied around today, Joy Junction is daily "ending" the contributory factors that cause homelessness—one life at a time—through its faith-based programs. We're finding that the need has never been greater. That's why we are preparing the way for much needed and long awaited new construction.

A short-term goal includes an expanded kitchen. Our current facility, while fully licensed and functional, was never intended to turn out well over 16,000 meals monthly. Our chef and his crew do a great job preparing balanced, nutritious, and attractively presented meals. But to do even better and keep up with what we believe will be an ever-increasing demand, expanded kitchen facilities are becoming a necessity.

Another thing important to our guests is a comfortable and designated children's area, where moms could go and "hang out" with their kids. While our multipurpose area is cool and safe, something more "kid friendly" would be wonderful. What a blessing it would be to have an expanded play area outside for the many youngsters who take refuge at Joy Junction with their parents. Play is important for child development, and with your prayers and support we can offer more to our young guests.

Something else important to recovery would be the provision of a computer lab for our guests. It's no secret that today's society is one where a working knowledge of computers is essential. While in a coffee shop recently, my eyes were drawn to the complex-looking computer screen being used by the barista to place a small food order and cups of coffee for my wife and me. It's not enough to just successfully make a caramel macchiato, a cappuccino, or a latte. A barista also needs to be able to handle the complex computer program. If we can provide some of that knowledge to our guests, we'll be giving them the edge they need to help them succeed. Next time you get your favorite coffee brew, sneak a peek at the computer if you can. You'll see what I mean.

We're also open to the possibility of expanding the concept and operating philosophy of Joy Junction to other communities around the United States.

So having said that, with the Lord as my guide and my wife Elma at my side (who contributed a number of the ideas listed above), I look forward to the next three decades helping the disenfranchised, marginalized, homeless and hungry. I hope you will consider joining us.

Food for Thought

"Where there is no vision, the people perish: but he that keepeth the law, happy is he" (29:18 KJV). I quoted this verse from the book of Proverbs at the beginning of this chapter.

Will you pray that God increases our discernment and sharpens our judgment about where we go and what we do to help the homeless? Will you pray that our vision and the fear of God combine to motivate us to obey the Lord? Your prayers would be the finest ministry you could offer to us.

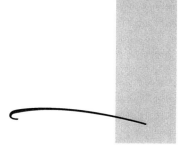

ABOUT THE AUTHOR

Jeremy Reynalds is a senior correspondent for the ASSIST News Service, a freelance writer, as well as the founder and CEO of Joy Junction, New Mexico's largest emergency homeless shelter, www.joyjunction.org. He has a master's degree in communication from the University of New Mexico and a Ph.D. in intercultural education from Biola University in Los Angeles. Reynalds lives in Albuquerque, New Mexico with his wife, Elma.

For more information contact: Jeremy Reynalds at jeremyreynalds@gmail.com.

For more information about Joy Junction,
please visit our website at
www.joyjunction.org
or
www.facebook.com/jjabq

P.O. Box 26561
Albuquerque, New Mexico 87125

CONTACT INFORMATION

REDEMPTION
PRESS

To order additional copies of this book, please visit
www.redemption-press.com.
Also available on Amazon.com and BarnesandNoble.com
Or by calling toll free 1-844-2REDEEM.

CPSIA information can be obtained
at www.ICGtesting.com
Printed in the USA
FSOW01n1616290716
23225FS

9 781683 140634